W9-ABM-469

Do Something

Do Something

Coming of Age
Amid the Glitter and Doom
of '70s New York

GUY TREBAY

ALFRED A. KNOPF New York
2024

THIS IS A BORZOI BOOK
PUBLISHED BY ALFRED A. KNOPF

www.aaknopf.com

Knopf, Borzoi Books, and the colophon are registered trademarks of Penguin Random House LLC.

Library of Congress Cataloging-in-Publication Data
Names: Trebay, Guy, 1952– author.
Title: Do something: coming of age amid the glitter
and doom of '70s New York / Guy Trebay.
Description: First edition. | New York: Alfred A. Knopf, 2024. |
Identifiers: LCCN 2023010445 (print) | LCCN 2023010446 (ebook) |
ISBN 9781524731977 (hardcover) | ISBN 9781524731984 (ebook)
Subjects: LCSH: Trebay, Guy, 1952– | Journalists—New York (State)—
New York—Biography. | New York (N.Y.)—Social life and customs—
20th century. | LCGFT: Autobiographies.
Classification: LCC PN4874.T67 A3 2024 (print) |
LCC PN4874.T67 (ebook) DDC 070.92 [B]—dc23/eng/20230804
LC record available at https://lccn.loc.gov/2023010445
LC ebook record available at https://lccn.loc.gov/2023010446

Jacket photograph by Scott Heiser, courtesy of the Estate of Scott Heiser
Jacket design by Chip Kidd

Manufactured in the United States of America
First Edition

For my siblings

Do Something

Much of that winter I spent kicking through the wreckage. Snowfall was unusually heavy that season and, trekking up the long driveway, I sometimes sank hip-deep into drifts, stumbling and lurching until, at the end of a curve, the remains of what had been my father's house came into view.

The chimneys were now blackened. The shell of the place was gone. The interior was left open to the elements. Wallpaper seared off in ice-glazed scrolls. With nothing visible to support it, a section of the second floor cantilevered into thin air.

People often say houses burn to the ground. In truth it doesn't work that way. Fire is a hungry and alive thing, devouring what it wants and brushing past what it can't be bothered to consume. Seeking fuel, the flames licked across a floor and up a stair leading to my little sister's room and then stopped. Everything around it was torched, yet her bedroom remained as though nothing had occurred. Her canopy bed was covered with a favorite patchwork star quilt, rumpled as if she'd just left it. Hanging above it was a lithograph of a red fox crouched atop a mossy hummock, lying in wait for two rabbits huddled below.

At the three windows overlooking what had been a dense hedge of yew bushes, curtains still hung from their rods, rigid ice flutes frozen in place. The view from those windows took in the trampled mounds of the bushes, which opened onto the broad rear yard, itself backed onto a hedge separating our property from that of an adjacent estate. The yews now resembled filthy bread loaves, blanketed in ash.

Part of the roof remained intact so, tenuous as it was, it provided me with some kind of cover as I prowled through the gutted remains. Here were the charred dining room chairs, their sleek modernist splats burnt to spearpoints; here, in the pantry, the homely Pfaltzgraff everyday dishes—relics of an earthy sixties phase of my mother's—stood molten together by heat in a lopsided accordion; here, an Italian modernist dining table my parents shipped home from Rome, its figured rosewood surface dulled with frost, legless and flat to the floor, bedded in a heap of soot.

What exactly I was looking for was not altogether clear. Much was destroyed or had been stolen. Vanished were the contents of a silver cabinet in the pantry that curiously remained otherwise intact. Its locked door had been pried and the contents of the shelves, with their linings of felted brown Pacific cloth, cleaned out thoroughly. I looked further to see what, if anything, was left behind from among those fancy, useless objects we possessed: the deep walnut box containing a seldom-used set of Gorham silverware in the King Edward pattern, presented to my parents on their engagement along with objects like a filigreed sterling Georgian cake basket; twelve stemmed silver goblets suggestive of a future in which, for a newly married couple barely in their twenties, sterling champagne coupes would be thought essential. Such were the things we had, and now there was nothing. Whatever the fire spared was carried off by firemen, who helped themselves to our stuff once the flames were out.

It surprised me at first to think that firemen steal. Later I would learn that it is not so unusual for things to walk away with the heroes in high boots. Some of what was taken had never amounted to much more than props suggestive of a life and class not ours to claim in the first place. Some of it may even have been "borrowed" from its original owners by the givers, though I could not know that then. Standing amid what was left of all that, I realized it no longer mattered.

Yet what weighed on me as I surveyed the scene was a sense of greater inevitability, as if the fire were a natural progression in a chain of disasters that occurred during a year of my life that stretched and compressed like a bellows, culminating in December 1975 with our house ablaze. So odd would these events seem in the retelling that I seldom mentioned them. In truth, I had begun to take for granted that a house that burns in the middle of a winter night was the sort of thing that happened to us.

The cause was straightforward. An ice storm striking the

East Coast had taken out electricity in a string of bay towns along the North Shore of Long Island. Manhattan, where I lived, had been unaffected. Sometime during the night power had flashed on and then abruptly gone dead, the surge strong enough to short old wires in a wall and, as they began to smolder and burn, to set the house alight. Its layout accounted, in a sense, for why certain parts burned while others were left unscathed. A low rambling structure built in the twenties as the gardener's cottage of a Gold Coast estate, the house had gradually expanded and been added to through the decades until it spread across three levels, a shingled up-and-down place, with additions that eventually stretched it to eighteen rooms—more if you counted a large garden shed and a care-taker's apartment above a garage converted from a carriage barn.

On the train from the city and then in a cab from the sta-tion I had already begun to feel as if made of lead. It was not sadness about the fire itself that weighed me down so much as a sense that, different from the placid lives I fantasized others having, in ours the conventional progression of familial mile-stones had been replaced by a parade of calamities.

What I had come looking for that day was a suitcase. Pebbled caramel leather with a rigid frame, saddle-stitched handles, and stiff leather bumpers at the corners, it had accompanied my mother for a brief stint at college and, when that dream was shelved in favor of marriage and motherhood, repurposed as photograph storage. Even empty the thing weighed a ton, and from its heft alone you could infer the existence of a world in which redcaps, bellmen, and porters were always on hand to carry your stuff.

Over a succession of weekends I had come looking for the case, trudging through the snow and then up the long driveway to what had been our red-painted door. My feet numbed quickly and, immediately upon entry, the acrid smoke smell caught in my nostrils. Ash stuck to the bottoms of my rubber-soled duck boots, and frozen vertical ridges formed in the seams of my jeans. While my sense of what the suitcase held was blurry, I recalled clearly a black-and-white snapshot of my mother carrying that very same suitcase to her all-girls Franciscan college in Joliet, Illinois. First in a graduated lineup of bright young women posed for a campus photographer, each with a valise at her feet, she was exceptionally and brightly pretty and more full-cheeked than she would ever again permit herself to be. In the style of a period when young women could not put girlhood behind them fast enough, she looked forty at eighteen.

They all did. Shiny-faced and with Lauren Bacall pageboys, wearing dark lipstick and an air of precocious maturity, her classmates in the photographs were lovely and somehow interchangeable. There had been plenty of pictures of my mother from those days and also from high school, a happy time for her, documented in dewy portrait poses and snapshots from the convent school she attended in Manhattan, images that confirmed what she was always too modest to mention, that she had been valedictorian of her class, captain of the drama and debate clubs, and the star of her swimming team.

That she was a beautiful swimmer was one fact impossible for her to downplay. Anatomically, she was built for the sport; at five feet eleven she was tall for her age—or for any woman in the 1940s—and with a broad, natural wingspan.

She had learned to swim in early girlhood from her older brother, Bud—if you can call it learning to be dragged into the Atlantic off the Maidstone Club beach in East Hampton and dumped into the surf.

"Anyway, it taught me not to drown," she once said, laughing and dragging on a Pall Mall. Yet what did she know of safety, she who had been raised without it, who had at the best of times known herself to be provisional, at least since that day when, age five or so, she and Bud had been sent temporarily by their unemployed parents to a charity institution in the Midwest—not an orphanage, because she was no orphan, but a "home" that can never have felt to her like any such thing. I can recall only once her mentioning that time as an abandonment that marked her for life.

Eventually my mother, the former Lucille Carole Foster, would pass along to me and my three siblings what she could of swimming, focusing on form and the long, easy strokes that, though natural to her, I could never master. Because we mostly swam in the Atlantic Ocean off Fire Island she also instructed us on how to survive a riptide, repeating the common wisdom about disciplining yourself to suppress the instinct to fight. Relax and release. Let the current carry you, no matter how far. Eventually, she explained, the force of the current will dissipate and weaken. Then you can make for shore.

I did learn to swim well enough, although I would not entirely lose my fear of the ocean, not in childhood or ever. My mother's fearlessness in the water passed me by, and I sometimes think perhaps she was less brave than indifferent to danger—as, in a way, both my parents were. Children raising children, they taught us few enough practical lessons, favoring instead a sense of boldness through action. While their timid friends bodysurfed the inshore waves, they would plow through head-high rollers and swim straight out as though headed for Portugal.

They had met when he was a young lifeguard at a City Island yacht and beach club where her school swim team sometimes went to practice. The Long Island Sound surf there was pathetic, they agreed, so in a borrowed car they sometimes drove to the ocean looking for whitecaps, slapping water on their flanks to adjust core temperature, high-stepping through the mush and diving beneath the first wave in a big set, then bobbing up to wait until another came along, one that, by unspoken signal, they agreed was worth riding.

Photos from their early years together show them almost always at beaches, in swimsuits, as though they hardly owned street clothes, tanned, and in my eyes burnished by a glamour that took a surprisingly long time to erode. Without question they were handsome people—she in the luscious manner of the brunette second-lead in an MGM movie, he a Mediterranean-indeterminate type like Victor Mature. Good looks were so important in their lives and in those of their friends and referred to so often that I mistook them for a value, as though to be less than attractive was a flaw of character. Only my mother's best friend from girls' school was exempted, based on her superior intelligence and a generalized sympathy for her as a Child of Divorce.

They posed an awful lot for the camera in those days with those friends. They posed on the coarse sand beach by a field-

Lucille Foster, Victor Trebay,
and unidentified friend circa 1947

stone wall erected where the baize-green clubhouse lawn abruptly stopped. The girls in their swimsuits stuck to the blankets, posed coyly, hugged their knees. The boys struck manly Charles Atlas poses with the Sound as their backdrop. They built human pyramids or stood silhouetted against the whitewashed walls of the changing cabanas, those long rows of booths with narrow aisles between them, their plank doors stenciled with anchors or sailing burgees; their interiors containing the inevitable bench and rows of wooden clothes pegs slung with damp suits, bathing caps decorated with appliqué daisies; and all the accumulated junk of beach summers, webbed folding chairs, deflated inner tubes, all of it imbued with the benzene smell of rubber overlaid with the musk and tang of salt-wet bodies.

All through early childhood we spent summers at the club, changing in cabana 41, which our family took year after year. Sometimes I would linger in that space after my parents had changed and hauled our towels and the beach chairs and a heavy, ice-filled plaid metal cooler down to the water. My sister, Laura—there were just two of us then, Irish twins, followed almost a decade later by another brother and sister—had nimbly swapped her street clothes for a stretchy swimsuit and run screaming for the water. In no hurry to shed my shorts and T-shirt, I sat quietly in the dim airless cabin, sunlight filtering through its planks, lost in thought until Laura came screaming up the boardwalk for me to join her in the water.

Unlike Laura, I never saw the beach as a place of pleasure. No matter how cold or rough the water, she threw herself in, dog-paddling to the diving float, well away from the lines and the buoy balls, unconcerned about the prehistoric horseshoe crabs lurking at the bottom with their rapier tails. The dogfish that came through seasonally, moving like swift and barely visible shadows beneath the surface, didn't bother her either. If she spotted a dorsal fin in the water, she sat awhile on the float until the shark swam away.

I, on the other hand, preferred to survey things from the beach—preferred, as it turned out in most things, to observe. I can recollect what a precocious reader I was, learning by sitting alongside my mother on our nubby 1950s living room sofa, nestled against her warmth, drinking in her blended smells of cigarettes and Ice-Blue Secret overlaid, if suppertime was near, with the Shalimar she dabbed on before my dad got home.

There, with the crisp pages of the Hay-Wingo phonics textbook opened between us, I thrilled to the sounds of letters taking shape as words, and in that memory I detected the origins of something obvious to me now, although which for a long time was difficult to see—that words became figures in patterns I arranged, that a word placed after a word and then another gave me power, an ability to make sentences and stories as a way of reconciling the divergence between the conventional and apparently placid surface of our family life, and realities I was not equipped to understand.

By now, back in the burnt-out house, my feet were ice blocks, yet I was determined to stick it out until I found the suitcase. Distractedly shuffling along the edge of what had been the kitchen pantry, I came close to dropping through a gap between floorboards and joists, pulling back before I plunged into the blackened void of the basement. Another step and I'd have dropped fifteen feet, and who then would have thought to look for me there? Embarrassed by my weird quest, I hadn't told anybody about these weekly trips. My archaeological mission having produced nothing, I suddenly felt deeply tired. Cold and exhausted and paranoid about falling, I inched slowly backward, hugging what had been a bedroom wall, when suddenly my bootheel struck something weighty. Instinctively I knew what it was. The suitcase had been there all along, of course, concealed by rubble from a collapsed chimney. Blistered and blackened, the surface looked broiled, yet the hasps were intact and, as I bent to open the thing on the snow-covered floor, the potential danger of this entire enterprise suddenly stopped me short.

Cautiously then, I humped it over the foundation as though dragging a body. I took it into a potting shed attached to a barn that had escaped the fire, hoisting it onto a thick wooden counter beneath a double-hung window overlooking a field.

This was a view I'd always loved, so undisturbed and placid, the panes of the window framing an old oak tree and a holly hedge now dusted with a confectionary coating of snow. It occurred to me then that I had made no provision for getting the suitcase home if I found it. It was too heavy to carry on a train and it stank of smoke. It was obvious I'd have to come back with a car, so I lifted aside a stack of mossed clay pots on a shelf beneath the ledge, maneuvering the suitcase as far back as I could manage, and shoved pots in front of it to hide it from view. Then I trudged back down the driveway and onto Vineyard Road to the crest of Cove Road, hugging the verge on switchbacks that snaked down to Halesite harbor. Cars tended to spin out here in icy conditions; getting flattened was not part of my plan.

The harbor was thick with ice, and dry-docked boats along the shoreline sat high in their wooden cradles. Shutting the door on the booth of a boatyard's solitary pay phone, I tugged a glove off my frozen fingers, fishing around in my parka for a dime to call a taxi. Suddenly, as I wiped condensate from the windows, I ached to be gone from here, to be seated on a hard leather bench seat on the Long Island Rail Road, feet thawing, headed home to my small studio apartment. Yet when I did board the train, sitting by a window dully marking a familiar litany of station stops—Cold Spring Harbor, Syosset, Hicksville, and then a series of anonymous bedroom towns in Nassau County—I felt myself pulled in a different direction, back and back to a past whose inhabitants, my own people, somehow felt to me like aliens.

It was springtime before I could fully recover the photos, months after I'd driven out and hauled the suitcase back to the city. While the fire had spared the pictures, the firemen's hoses hadn't; soaked and fused, the prints were mostly sodden clumps. Eventually, through trial and error, I figured out how to peel them apart using water-filled plastic dishpans, giving each a first rinse and then another in sequence, being careful to extract them from the water as soon as they floated free of one another, before they could disintegrate. No matter how often I changed the water, each retained the stench of smoke, a smell that permeated everything, clung to my skin, becoming so much a part of me that people in stores began to shoot me weird looks. I kept at it, though, bathing and gently pry-ing apart the fused pictures, blotting them with paper towels before sliding each between the pages of books weighted with rocks.

A memory recurs, from this time, of a small black-and-white snapshot—an image I studied minutely before figuring out that what it depicted was my uncle Reginald's DeSoto. By squinting I could make out a figure behind the wheel; it was my mother. She was wearing oversize sunglasses and a striped terry-cloth beach shift and gesturing animatedly to someone unseen. I love this photo and I loved that car, prob-ably best of all those we had in the money years, back when my father's business was booming, before a business partner swindled the company out from under him, when we could still fool ourselves into imagining the money would be there forever. There was a Cadillac Coupe de Ville for my father, the model with modified shark-fin taillights, a black leather interior, a light-up console in custom rosewood. There was a red convertible MG with a fold-down vinyl roof; and another Cadillac, which model I can't recall; and a Jaguar XK-E slung so low my father had to shoehorn himself behind the wheel. There was a six-seater white Oldsmobile Vista Cruiser station wagon with a bump-out roof and clerestory windows, a fea-ture of no obvious practical purpose in a vehicle with almost as much glass as steel.

The Olds was the family car, my mom's regular ride, intended for errands and supermarket runs and technically also for trips to the beach. Yet for those we preferred the 1948 DeSoto, handed down by a paternal uncle, a strange man with a bald dome, a papery complexion, and a Roman nose. Reginald, called Rene, lived in a snug brick house in Plandome Manor with his mother, a woman then in her nineties, a tiny human habitually dressed in flower-print frocks and lace-up shoes with leather-covered heels, a figure so remote and generally wordless that I wondered, as a child, whether she was mute.

Rene shared that house and its enveloping silences with my great-grandmother and with Chipper, an ancient wire-haired terrier that was the latest in a succession of similar pets all bearing the same name. When, in the early 1970s, Rene died and his home was besieged by family members searching for what loot they could grab before the house was sealed for probate, myself and my siblings and a cousin were set free to raid closets and cabinets, ransacking them for weird unguents and dated furs, stuff we were encouraged to take if we wished. Laura, I recall, grabbed a mink stole, one of those sinister capelets that fastened with sharp-toothed mink heads snapping at their own tails. My cousin chose a man's Omega dress watch found in a dresser, a delicate timepiece with a ladylike dial. I was unsure what to keep until, after we'd searched all the bedrooms, closets, and cupboards, I slipped away from the others and crept up the attic stairs.

It took a while for my eyes to adjust to the light in that still space full of trunks and broken-bottomed cane chairs, the castoffs of two long lives, the piles of *National Geographic* magazines stacked waist high. It seemed unpromising to me until—in a corner where the roofline canted steeply and tucked behind some steamer trunks plastered with stickers from the Hamburg-America, the Cunard, and the French lines—I fell upon the sight of a small pack of five former Chippers, mounted and stuffed.

Somehow the existence of these taxidermy specimens struck me as no odder than anything else about that place. Somehow, too, it did not occur to me for a long time that the moth-eaten terrier I took home that day, with its cracked ears and following eyes, was part of a larger and less tangible inheritance. Like so much else from that time, I dragged Chipper around for years, from one room or apartment to another, not certain why and yet always finding a space for this threadbare relic, less because it meant anything to me than because getting rid of it, or of the memories it somehow evoked, was more effort than keeping it around.

Although the DeSoto was over a decade old by the time we got it, the odometer barely registered twenty thousand miles. This was the mark at which Rene retired his automobiles and bought new ones. Though he often traded the old model, this was passed along or sold to my dad, who immediately gave it to my mother to become our beach car, a beloved humpbacked behemoth colored the iridescent blue of a shell, its interior so cavernous the younger kids could stand up inside. Seasons of swimsuit wet had corrupted the plush upholstery, leaving it smelling of salt and mildew and so stiff that the rough cloth sandpapered your thighs when you perched on the edge of the seat.

Running boards were the car's standout feature: twin exterior hardboards extending from rear to front wheel guards, covered in ribbed rubber and trimmed in chrome. Though they were designed as steps up to the unusually high cab, we used them mostly as platforms for our thrill rides to the beach. Arms circled through the open windows of the doorframe, bare feet clinging to hot rubber, wind flattening our hair, we took turns riding on the running board when my mom let us, which was most of the time. She worked the gearshift with her right hand, the left one steadying the wheel while simultaneously cradling a "ciggie" between index and middle fingers.

What did she sound like? I strain to recall. Nowadays, for no good reason, I preserve voice mails, but back then the technology was nonexistent; what's more, it never occurred to me how quickly the tone and timbre of a loved one's voice evaporates. Mostly what I am left with is her gestures, the most typical the most mechanical, that of a hand reaching for the day's first smoke as we kids stopped at the bedroom to say goodbye before school. It would be reassuring to think of her as someone who fixed us hearty breakfasts or poured milk over our cornflakes, but I am content enough to recall her fumbling for a bedside pack and matches to light up that first rapturous smoke.

My mother smoked Pall Malls, each cigarette a link in a continuous chain stretching back to her girlhood, that point at around fourteen when she learned to light up. At first it was Lucky Strikes ("It's toasted!") cadged from her brother and then afterward Camels and finally and forever afterward the medium-filter Pall Malls in the stiff red pack, the one with the flip top and a cellophane wrapper that could be used as a makeshift ashtray in a pinch. It was those cigarettes she let us try in an attempt to scare us off the habit, and that she used to demonstrate how to inhale and also to make a guppy mouth and use your cheeks as bellows for blowing out perfect smoke rings.

With her palm flat on the wheel, our mom would cruise down to the beach club past all the big houses tucked into the low hills of our incorporated village—past the FitzMaurice place, with its blue-ceilinged porch; past the Watson pile half-hidden behind privets; past spooky Boylancrest Farms, largest of all the piles surrounding us, a mysterious and forlorn brick behemoth with its curtains drawn, its clay tennis courts fissured, its broad lawns cut weekly by a gardener hauling a utility trailer bristling with shovels and rakes. Why, I do not know, but when the gardener mowed, he preserved a wide circle around each of the Wagnerian statues mounted on plinths across the property, statues long since decapitated by vandals, armless and headless, the high grass around them like crime-scene silhouettes outlining what was left of Siegfried, Wotan, and Alberich.

There is no contesting the fact that other people's mothers were less offhand about ferrying their kids around on the exterior of the family automobile. Yet other people's mothers were boring. They did not, as ours seemed to do, consider it a prime element of parental responsibility to foster daring in their kids. And it never occurred to her, as it undoubtedly did to our neighbors, that we were outliers who in all likelihood had no business living in that place and among that class of people whose surnames tended to be emblazoned on everyday products, the kind Fitzgerald had in mind when he said that fortune comes to them comfortably early and easy.

We were interlopers, yes, although not quite impostors. My parents were nicely brought-up people, yet too guileless and uncynical to apply themselves to the hard work of social climbing. Maybe "impersonators" is the word since for them it was enough to live expansively, as though they had always had a great deal of money, and if they had an aptitude for this it owed in part to the fluke of my mother having passed her girlhood among the wealthiest Americans in Tuxedo Park.

It was there, in a walled and gated tycoon's playground, a fantasy realm of Norman keeps and half-timbered Tudor manors and French châteaux set among the hills of Orange County in upstate New York, that she lived from about the age of six—when she'd been rescued from the charity home once her parents regained their bearings—until the time came for her to lug her heavy leather suitcase off to college.

There is another picture I salvaged during that winter of 1975, a period when by rights I should have been partying or finding a career or fucking around but instead I'd spent preserving images saved from the fire, pressing them into a leather-bound album unearthed at a thrift shop, its pristine pages still interleaved with gossamer tissue paper. As I arranged and affixed these snapshots to the pages, unconsciously I was setting about inventing sequences in a narrative that, even as I composed it, I must inwardly have known to be false. The photograph I am thinking about depicts a small family: my mother; her brother, Bud; and their parents, seated on the stone steps of a terrace below which slopes a broad lawn. Standing behind them is an imposing baronial manor, rusticated and many-chimneyed, magisterial in silhouette and

Tuxedo Park

so large in its footprint that its roofline is uneven, reflecting the amount of ground it covers. Though the image is small, I count eighteen windows across the facade, one lighting a deep bay, another graduated set looking like panpipes, a third forming a bay with a conical roof like a stage-set whimsy from a comic operetta.

Though the figures are indistinct, I can clearly make out my grandparents and my mother, who is seated and with a dog at her side. I wonder whose animal this is, though, since I never knew her to mention a pet, and I wonder, too, whether the dog was not a prop borrowed for a grouping so naturally composed that any viewer might assume this grand mansion overlooking this trimmed lawn, and with this terrace shaded by large petaled umbrellas, is the domain of the people in the photographs. Yet it wasn't my grandparents' home. Someone else owned it. And as for the big white Packard touring car featured in another photograph—the one where my grand-father stands leaning against the hood in his natty white gab-ardine suit and wearing his smartly creased Borsalino—that wasn't theirs, either.

In those days, just after the Great Depression, when jobs were so hard to come by that millions were forced onto bread-lines, this man I never met and about whom I picked up, in childhood, little more than some random biographical scraps—that, for instance, when still a teenager in Columbus, Ohio, he had lied about his age to enlist in the Army during the First World War; that he had been gassed in the trenches with xylyl bromide; that despite a hero's medal, he was jobless on his return and for a time ran bootleg liquor—had finally found employment as the driver for an exceptionally rich man. Although much later he would graduate to a series of mid-level executive positions at Metropolitan Life Insurance head-quarters, in those early days his job required him to wear livery. When I think of this man of nearly six feet seven, impressively handsome in his even-featured Anglo way, it is easy to imag-ine the flush of humiliation he would experience slipping on a jacket and chauffeur's cap, to think of him as a spectacle, an elegant giant opening car doors.

The job had its perks. Among these was a house on the grounds of the Tuxedo Park estate, an apartment above that family's carriage house on East Sixty-Eighth Street, and the chance to trail his employers on their seasonal migrations. Thus it is that my mother learned to swim not at the pub-lic beach in East Hampton but at a stretch of ocean adjacent to the Maidstone Club; and to play tennis on clay courts at

Orson Dallas Foster, my maternal grandfather, in driver's seat

Tuxedo Park; and for her brother to pick up the arcane game of court tennis, a sport limited then and now by the number and location of places where it is practiced, never more than ten courts in the country, most located at private men's clubs or on the grounds of great private estates. This is how my mother absorbed half-unconsciously and, it would seem, transmitted to us, a knowledge of folkways particular to the upper class. And it is why, even after our family existed as little more than a collection of scattered genetic puzzle pieces, on the rare occasions when we came together the table was properly set for dinner, why decks of playing cards and scorepads were laid out at rigid right angles on a leather-topped table used only for bridge, and why roast beef was always carved to the thinness of paper.

I must have known all along, as I glued the salvaged images into album pages, that I was perpetuating a fiction since little of the stuff depicted—the mansion, the limousine, what looks to be a spaniel in the photo of my mother and her family—belonged to the man with the two-tone spectator shoes proprietarily propped on the tire of a shiny white Packard. That man, my grandfather, and his family, my mother's people, are the help.

o o o

ON A HANGTAG strung around every bottle of the men's cologne that was the unlikely source of my dad's astonishingly runaway, if short-lived, success was inscribed a legend: "For the use of manly descendants in spirit, of a special breed of adventurer." The cologne, the legend, the whole enterprise was the brainchild of a man prosaically raised in the Bronx, educated at parochial boys' schools, and employed, when he started his own company, as an account manager for *Parade* magazine; and whose general approach to adventure was to bet your money before his own.

This was certainly the case when he built an inspired and risky little start-up on a grubstake seeded by raiding his children's college funds. It would not be until much later, when the money was long gone, that we learned how blithely, to start Hawaiian Surf, my dad had mined the modest trusts our grandmothers had put away for us. By then my siblings and I were scattered in all directions, with barely a high school diploma between us.

The others adjusted to this variously, of course—that is, if ever they became aware of it. I am not so certain they did.

Laura, my closest sibling, had already gone so far off the rails by her junior year of high school that the general aim of keeping her out of jail outran whatever ambitions my parents may have had for her ongoing education. With eight years separating us, my two other siblings moved in a separate orbit; as far as we were concerned, they tracked the sun of a far-off solar system. It was only a lot later that I could see them as my blood relations and not two hapless souls accidentally lodging under the same roof. As for me, any expectation that I would pursue higher education dwindled so steadily that I barely stumbled through high school, striking out on my own at seventeen without bothering to collect my diploma.

But that would all be in the future. I was still a directionless adolescent when my dad began siphoning savings from our grandmothers into the creation of a "groovy" men's cologne and associated product line that would make a marked imprint on sixties culture and also make us rich for a while. Hawaiian Surf came in a cork-wrapped bottle, the design stroke that distinguished it in an increasingly crowded market, and had a marine-blue label adorned with a compass rose. I would put the life span at no more than a decade for this product, which sold "in the millions" at retailers around the country, as a trade journal breathlessly reported at the time, its sales flogged relentlessly by my father during a near-constant succession of road trips. It was available at "fine retailers everywhere," as another article noted—"everywhere" in this case including Canada, Australia, South America, and Mexico, where the upscale Sanborn chain became and remained one of my father's biggest "doors."

Impressive as his overnight success was, it never became clear how my father had pulled off the feat of taking a clever, low-budget concept and muscling it past industry stalwarts like Old Spice, with its yeasty fragrance and 1930s milk-glass bottle; or foreign imports like English Leather or even Playboy-era novelties like Hai Karate—a cologne so primitive in its approach to the seduction that is the putative reason to wear cologne in the first place that it came with printed instructions for fighting off women driven mad by the scent. To us kids the stuff all smelled more or less equally awful. The exception was Brut, whose poison-green Essence of Man had the noxious tang of bug spray, with heady top notes of sandalwood and oak moss.

The five rings of cork encasing each Hawaiian Surf bottle came in crates from Portugal and, at the beginning, these were delivered to us at home, wrapped in hemp bales, along with boxes of miniature cork rings for use in making samples. It did not occur to anyone for a second to think of it as child labor when we kids were recruited to soak and soften the rings in a bathtub before threading them onto tiny flacons. It was more like a family game. The flacons would go off to be filled afterward, distributed free as samples, and we all felt an element of proprietary pride when—perhaps boosted by a burgeoning surf culture—the goofy product with its cork rings, its neocolonialist theme, its sweetish citric fragrance, took off.

Suddenly what had begun as a way for my father to escape a deadening climb up a corporate ladder became a viable business. And just as abruptly he was able—despite having four young mouths to feed—to quit his day job and become a player in the cutthroat perfume trade. Simultaneously we were inducted into the mysteries of worlds that seemed incredibly arcane to us, our TV room filling up with surfboards and opaque glass quarts of fragrances that, bottled and packaged as Guerlain's Mitsouko or Jean Patou's Eau de Joy, were advertised even then as "the most expensive perfume in the world." It was potent stuff, and it all happened so quickly that my dad got drunk on the hype. "If you take one hundred twenty of the sixteen-ounce bottles and lash them together," he told a credulous trade reporter, "you've got a raft that will carry you to Hawaii."

It goes without saying that no connection existed between my father's invention and the complex social and cultural realities of Hawaii. In fact, there was nothing at all linking the product to islands that had only just achieved US statehood. From the outset Hawaiian Surf was bottled, assembled, packed, and shipped from a squat forty-thousand-square-foot factory in an industrial park on the South Shore of Long Island. Eventually another would be built to produce the stuff, just over the border from Mexico in the hot and dusty Sonoran desert town of Nogales, Arizona.

Once, or maybe twice, Laura and I got to tag along with our father to his office in Deer Park, a glassed-in suite just off the factory floor where, in surly teen fashion, we snooped around the plant as assembly-line workers in lab coats and hairnets soaked the cork rings, fed the bottles into a machine that applied them, topped off the now-hidden glass cylinders with pale amber liquid, and capped them, loaded the results on what looked like vast bakery racks for drying, and then fed them into labeling machines before they were moved onto conveyor belts leading to heat tunnels to be covered in shrink-wrap.

It happens that, somewhat later in my life, I would cross large stretches of the frigid North Atlantic as a crew member on a forty-five-foot sailboat. It never occurred to me then to think of myself as in any way linked to the stalwart "special breed" my dad made his fortune conjuring up, "men of courage, dignity, and with a lust for adventure," the type that might "cross the uncharted vastness of the Pacific in search of Paradise." And if I ever met anyone of that kind, I surely did not know it.

As for paradise itself—well, as far as we could tell it came packaged in four-, eight-, and sixteen-ounce bottles at Macy's, along with other elements of a product line that included scented talcum powder, stick deodorant, and an insistently phallic-looking soap on a rope. Not long ago I chased down some vintage Hawaiian Surf on eBay, attempting without success to find a shrink-wrapped virgin bottle. Though I never did, I occasionally scored bottles containing dregs of the fragrance; unscrewing the caps to inhale the citrusy aroma, I waited for memories that refused to be triggered, and instead found myself contemplating how hard we sometimes work to recapture moments that, in fact, may never have occurred.

Well into his nineties my father wrote snail-mail letters. Since he lived in another city, I never saw the desk he referred to as his landfill and on which he composed, or assembled, missives that were collages of his hen scratch and newspaper clippings and metallic stickers, indecipherable and barely worth saving for their contents, yet precious to me for their envelopes and the labels he affixed to the upper left-hand corner. These were the kind often sent as promotions by charitable entities like Amnesty International or Doctors without Borders—causes that, as a confirmed Fox News viewer, my father could not plausibly have supported. Though he had little enough in the bank by then to allow for charitable donations, he perhaps mailed off the occasional mite to guarantee a steady supply of personalized labels bearing a return street address in a stolid Baltimore neighborhood beneath the name of an entirely imaginary person: Kent Kahumoku, a Hawaiian prince.

Who besides me got letters addressed by this fantasy person? What could those letters possibly have said? I used to be ashamed of the mythologies my dad quilted together from James Michener novels or *Hawaii Five-O*, priggishly making it my business to bone up on the lineages of the Polynesian sovereigns, on the missionary colonizers, on the sugar barons' greedy predations, on archaic navigational techniques employed by contemporary voyaging societies or the names of *kumu hula* said to have a direct line to Madame Pele, the volcano goddess.

I feel differently now. I see my dad's fantasy selves as an alternate form of wayfinding, a Sunday comics manner of journeying outward from the inner landscapes of a petted yet emotionally impoverished kid who dreamed his way into realms far removed from the stuffy Bronx railroad apartment where he lived until marriage: East 183rd Street, Apartment 1, first door on the left past a vestibule, two street-facing windows with a dreary prospect, nothing more exciting within range than the commercial strip of Fordham Road.

A solitary kid, from what I can make out, my dad was rendered fatherless by a car accident that occurred when he was seventeen. He was distant enough in age from his two older sisters to have grown up anyway as a spoiled boychild, my grandmother's one son, unselfconscious about being called the Little Prince. Once or twice I visited my grandmother in that apartment, and what remains with me from those times is the gravitational weight of rooms where furniture and objects are never moved from their positions, of spaces whose main function is arresting time. If, as Thomas McGuane wrote, it is true that we spend our lives trying to understand our parents, I can look compassionately on dear Prince Kent Kahumoku chasing the shadow of his vanishing father, into a theater of his own making, a play in which he not only enacts all the roles but is his own most adoring audience.

In the years when it would have made any functional difference, my glamorous and flamboyant dad was for his own children at best a careless and intermittently available figure. What he produced most consistently for the entertainment, if not quite benefit, of those around him was a stellar performance. In an odd and coincidental way, I see now that this prepared me to come of age in Manhattan during a period when, as it would happen, the city was populated by an awful lot of people whose sole driving ambition was reinventing themselves.

One of many Miss Hawaiian Surfs

∘ ∘ ∘

I AM IN THE BACK SEAT of my father's Cadillac, and I am twelve. He and I are headed to an in-store demonstration at Macy's Roosevelt Field. On the channeled leather bench front seat with my dad sits Miss Hawaiian Surf, one among a number of lovely if somewhat interchangeable paid performers, women my father has described in trade journals, with the blithely benighted attitude of the time, as fitting a fixed stereotype: "Long black hair, pretty muumuus," and with the ability, if called upon, to perform some version of a hula.

Theoretically, each Miss Hawaiian Surf is provided for her in-store gig with a flowered dress and lei. Yet since it is next to impossible in mid-1960s Long Island or Milwaukee or Baton Rouge to procure fresh maile leaves or pikake blossoms, most Miss Hawaiian Surfs make do with cheap silk replicas. It occurs to me that somehow this Miss Hawaiian Surf must be special since her lei is a real one, made from twined white tuberose blossoms that fill the car with their heady scent.

At the mall, we park in the lot, and wend our way to the men's department, an odd-looking trio: this man in a gabardine suit and tie, a young boy in khakis, and a young woman with a wool coat worn over a grass skirt. Inside Macy's we thread the aisles to a counter, where a manager helps my dad set up for his demo near an endcap where a cork surfboard stands propped against a large photoprint of Waikiki.

Ducking behind a gleaming chrome-and-glass counter to shed her street shoes, Miss Hawaiian Surf waits for my father to make his sales pitch to a gathering of customers. It is the

usual spiel about intrepid men of adventure. Slowly, distractedly, I drift away from the crowd and watch from a distance
as, at some point, a tape recorder is brought out and someone presses a button to play ukulele music, and Miss Hawaiian Surf moves to the front of the crowd and undulates, for
a while, in what even I can tell is an ersatz interpretation of
Hawaiian dance.

On our ride there, Miss Hawaiian Surf had talked about
her background, explaining for me that she was a first-
generation American of Puerto Rican ancestry, that she had
grown up in Yonkers and trained as a dancer, and that she
had big show-business ambitions—goals even a twelve-year-
old understood were unlikely to follow from department-store
gigs. Still, I supposed that she must be a talented dancer just
as I supposed that the customers enjoyed the performance.
If I did, too, it was because I was thrilled to find myself in
this adult setting, a stagehand ready with her coat when Miss
Hawaiian Surf finished her dance and clicked off the tape
recorder and the customers crowded the counter to purchase
product in a way that made me giddy since, until this moment,
I had never connected my father's business with anything like
actual commerce.

Afterward we packed up and returned to the Cadillac,
loaded the props in the trunk, and slid into our seats. With
the adults up front again, I wedged into the back seat between
the lei, now returned to the florist's box, and a door over which
Miss Hawaiian Surf had hung her grass skirt from a hook.
Speeding along the Southern State Parkway, we motored back
to the factory in Deer Park and, as we did, I practiced squint-

ing at a landscape that seemed subaqueous when viewed through the fronds, drifting along submerged in a dreamy state, half conscious of the intimate adult laughter and some private understanding between the two people up front.

The tuberose blossoms in the box beside me had begun to exude a sweet-smelling fragrance that would eventually decompose and release a chemical compound whose odor resembles ordure. Gradually, I sensed that the physical distance between Miss Hawaiian Surf and my father was closing, and with that realization came a revised perception about what I had excitedly thought of as a rare father-son excursion. Looking back now at the odd and vigilant kid I was, I can also see the stirrings of a lifelong attention to motive. Perennially distracted as a student, I was nonetheless watchful and given to parsing people's actions for their underlying intentions and equally determined, in my unformed way, to be nobody but myself in a world that, as someone once said, day and night does its best to make you into everybody else. Looking at it now, I also date to that moment the beginnings of what would become my vocation. That is, I saw the plot. I had been brought along that day as a beard.

o o o

WE ARE AT HOME. It is a humid and lush green summer in the low hills of Long Island's North Shore. Two years have passed since that trip to Roosevelt Field. I am now fourteen. On the road a lot of the time, my father leaves the running of the household to my mom, overwhelmed by the job of raising—if that is the word—four kids while managing a large house and maintaining the facade of a marriage that is not now, and perhaps never was, much more for her than a kind of glorified indenture. By now my dad has taken into the booming business a partner, a man I'll refer to as Mert Winters, an amiable, chunky character with a trustworthy face and about the last person you might take for the embezzler he will eventually turn out to be. Mert and his wife, Judith, have somehow become my parents' new best friends, the couple as close as I can recall to a regular presence around the house. They make an unlikely quartet since, while my parents are sporty and stylish, Mert and Judith are lumpen and stereotypically suburban—or hipster-suburban to be more precise, given their anomalous and unlikely love of country music.

I cannot say how they met in the first place or what Mert Winters's connection may have been to the fragrance or to any other industry, or even where they lived. Yet suddenly these people were in our lives. The couples planned vacations together. They double-dated at Bond films. They drank Harvey Wallbangers and listened to "controversial" Smothers Brothers albums and danced in our living room to vinyl records from my parents' collection, music so far from the Yardbirds records I listened to that it sent me retreating to the farthest rooms of the house.

Judith was olive-skinned and petite, had long center-parted brunette hair. She put me in mind of Buffy Sainte-Marie, yet Judith was no Buffy Sainte-Marie fan, could not have given a shit about broken treaties or land thefts from the Seneca or the Navajo Long Walk, and was about as far as you could get from the "dear lady" Sainte-Marie bitterly addressed in her quavering folkie plaint "Now That the Buffalo's Gone." In Judith's view, from what I could make out, bleeding-heart liberals were stooges. She and Mert preferred hillbilly music to all other strains of country, liked it for the flash-card morality of its soap-opera plotlines, liked it because they could go aurally slumming in a landscape of cheating hearts and honky-tonk angels and sucker outcomes. Others' misfortunes, both in song and in life, seemed to amuse the Winterses, and for that fairly simple reason, they viewed most people, my parents included, as marks.

Not altogether surprisingly, Judith was charming and seemed naturally to fold others into her confidence. One of her schemes, the first with consequences for me, begins. She and my mother sit over midmorning coffee in the breakfast room of the big house, chairs pulled up to a kitchen table customized by my mom, during a period of misguided hobby-ism, with awful, patterned floor tiles glued to the surface.

Judith has a plan. The plan involves a charitable aid service that funnels domestic workers from Central America to the United States. Flush with Hawaiian Surf money, my parents decide to hire a second housekeeper to assist the agency-hired live-in who does the daily basics, a Jamaican woman at once intensely pious and subversive enough to trick us kids into sniffing from a perfume bottle that turned out to contain smelling salts.

Here in the prosperous suburbs things are different from New York City, where, as I later learned, it was not unusual for people to wait at the Port Authority and hire their household help straight off buses arriving hourly from the Deep South. Judith's connection has a pipeline to Central America; focusing on whatever unstable country was in the worst shape, agency workers fanned out and recruited young women, ostensibly for domestic work though just as likely for something resembling human trafficking, an outcome that was not at the time an automatic consideration. El Salvador was then in a state of near economic collapse and political turmoil, so of course that was where the recruiters focused. "I've already put in my request," Judith says, as though she were ordering monogrammed party napkins from Lillian Vernon. "You should, too."

The transaction was implausibly straightforward. The process took almost no time at all. In just under two months, my parents and their four kids and the stout, churchy woman who ran our house would be living in close quarters and on intimate terms with a total stranger, a woman whose image we had conjured up from a misleading application photo and equally some not-so-innocently willed clichés. We—or, anyway, I—envisioned this person, Marta, as a country girl dressed in simple cotton clothing and with her hair chastely covered with a chin-tied rebozo, a picture consistent with the childish misapprehension most white Americans of the 1960s held of anyone residing outside US borders.

Whatever the source of my preconceived notions about Marta's appearance, they were shattered by the apparition that swiveled out of customs at Kennedy Airport on the day of arrival, a buxom young woman in a cocktail dress with a nipped waistline, patent-leather stilettos, and her hair styled in a high lacquered beehive. Marta's eyes were heavily made up, and she was carrying a cheap suitcase my mother grabbed as my father hustled off to the parking lot for his Coupe de Ville.

Can Marta's shock have been any less than our own, as we drove in silence across Long Island on the expressway, exiting at Syosset to cut past a swath of tract-house suburbs opening out after Route 25A to the monied shore towns rimming Long Island Sound, places like Locust Valley, Oyster Bay, Oyster Bay Cove, Laurel Hollow, Cold Spring Harbor, and, just beyond them, our little village of Huntington Bay, with its clipped lawns and hilly lanes and signposts hung with placards indicating residents' names and warning intruders that this was a Private Incorporated Village, regularly patrolled?

The room prepared for Marta was at the end of a long hallway leading from a butler's pantry. Depositing her suitcase, my mother showed her the adjacent bathroom and offered her a glass of water, and, just like that, an as yet undetectably pregnant young immigrant from the capital of a chronically unstable Central American country became a citizen of our precarious and alien household. What I have failed to note so far is that Mert and Judith were also at the airport that day to meet their new housekeeper, a woman who conformed exactly to the stereotype we'd had of Marta. Squat and sturdy, with a gold cap covering one front tooth, Yolanda was in gesture and attire the antithesis of Marta, whose manicure alone made it obvious—as if it was not already—that housekeeping was not her customary line of work.

Still, for a time she went through the motions. Or she did

until what turned out to be her second trimester, by which time the implications of her increasing bouts of moody indisposition had become too obvious to ignore. When morning sickness set in, there was whispered adult talk about what could be done. All the while Marta continued to clean in a desultory way, no longer dressed in stilettos, but spending her increasingly long breaks glued to a Motorola TV set on a tray stand in her room. Every Thursday my mother drove her to the station to catch a train to the city. Nobody knew where she went.

Marta's room was located on the end of the house far from my own. Even though reaching her quarters required me to traverse the library, foyer, living and dining rooms, a pantry, and that long hallway also leading to a seldom-used auxiliary cellar, I began to hang around Marta like a pubescent puppy. At first I was tentative about this, and then increasingly bold and stupid; in my adolescent misreading, her occasional glances my way felt like an invitation. I spent more and more time mooning on the threshold of Marta's room and—while it is not unthinkable that she'd given some thought to seducing me as a desperate ploy to escape an increasingly untenable situation—there is no justification for whatever urged me to turn up at her door one late evening expectantly.

Looking back at this nonincident, I suppose I expected her to call this virginal nincompoop to her bed. That, of course, did not happen. What I remember most clearly from that frozen moment is how a night-light near Marta's bed illuminated her heart-shaped face, and a beehive protectively swaddled in a nimbus of toilet paper. I remember Marta calmly and quietly assessing things before suddenly opening her mouth to emit a horror-movie wail, a banshee sound that followed me like a contrail as I raced, panting, down the hall through all the rooms of the ground floor.

Soon after that, Marta vanished forever. Before this happened, she would fling herself down a modest set of stairs in an unsuccessful effort to miscarry. Before this happened, she would return on the train from a visit to Manhattan to what we by then assumed was a boyfriend. Wearing a necklace of hickeys on her neck and a conspicuous bruise on one cheek, Marta remained in our house for another week and then was gone; we learned from Yolanda, by way of Judith, that the boyfriend, or whatever he was, had come for her in his car.

Like so many other events in our young lives, this one passed without explanation. The morning after my visit to Marta's room, I naturally expected a parental reaction, but that did not happen. All night long I had sat up dreading the morning, yet when it came things went on precisely as normal, my siblings and I wolfing the breakfasts prepared by the Jamaican housekeeper, and then dashing down the long drive to get the school bus.

I don't remember seeing Marta that next morning or the two of us ever again making eye contact. I know now that Marta at the time was probably less than a decade older than me, that she had come to this country fleeing a bad situation only to find another one waiting. My parents could hardly have known this at the time, and yet, as when faced with so many other practicalities, they reacted with passive bewilderment, little more equipped to help Marta than they ever would their own children. And in that one sense Marta and I turned out to be as alike as different. When eventually she blew town for good, my parents were elated by what must have seemed the logical end to a failed undertaking. Like the puppies my dad sometimes brought home from pet shops or breeders and handed off to shelters once they began making messes, Marta was always destined to disappear. And it was not long after she vanished that I turned fifteen, learned to drive, lost my virginity, and started to fuck around in earnest.

Then began a summer when I took to tripping on acid and whatever other hallucinogens I could lay my hands on, and screwing around as often as possible. My initiation into sex took place in a family car in a parking circle adjacent to a screened porch off my bedroom, a room attached to a wing of the house connected by a small passageway to the paneled and painted library. This suite of rooms, also some distance from those of my parents and siblings, overlooked a graveled circle hemmed by a yew hedge demarcating a boundary between our property and that of the neighboring estate. Mourning doves roosted in the yews and it is their murmurs I recall best, a chorus accompanying the whimpers of the girl I lose my virginity to, a seventeen-year-old from my high school sprawled across the seat of her father's Volvo.

She is not anyone I know well, a friend of a friend I get stoned with at a party, and who later offers to drive me home. What I remember most clearly from this debut is an awkward sense of putting on a performance, a feeling that will hardly change over the decades to come, whether it happens that my partners in bed will be high school pals or adult lovers of either sex. In almost every circumstance the sense I will have is of detachment, as though my body exists distinct from consciousness with me hovering somewhere above and outside it.

Neither of us on that autumn night was aware we had attracted an audience. It was early when we'd left the party, perhaps ten o'clock, and though we coasted up the drive with the lights out my kid brother, Glenn, heard us and crept out with a couple of sleepover pals, a nosy, seven-year-old search party. As I humped away clumsily the windows fogged, and then suddenly three boys were banging on the side panels. Yanking up my jeans, I jammed my hard-on back in my trousers, jumped from the car, and chased them across a field, the three kids laughing and shrieking. By the time I returned, the girl in the Volvo had already torn down the driveway and out of my life and, while I wish I could remember what her name was, like so much else from the time, that detail is irrecoverably lost.

In a newspaper clipping my dad kept in his files, I once encountered his assertion that he and my mother traveled on Hawaiian Surf business thirty weeks of the year. It was a typical exaggeration, although not quite a lie. "We try to get back on weekends whenever we can to be with our four youngsters," my father added, though of course the reality was that he was often on the road while my mother was left at home to start drinking too often, too early in the day as a way of easing the bleak realization that she'd been marooned with four kids by a husband who saw us all about as often as a house sitter does when the owner stops by for the mail.

Gabrielle Hamilton once observed that, by the time her own parents realized they had abandoned their children, "we were not to be recovered." You could convincingly make the same statement of Laura and me as we took to skipping out of school, smoking weed all the time with our stoner buddies, treating the house as a way station between trips to Manhattan to score pot, or else to the Walt Whitman Mall, where few of the upper-middle-class residents of our neighborhood deigned to go shopping (for their pastel corduroys and boiled-wool Bleyle jackets and Pappagallo flats and wooden-handled Bermuda bags with changeable monogrammed covers, there was the Hitching Post in Cold Spring Harbor) and where we ransacked the record and department stores, shoplifting anything that wasn't nailed down.

For part of one season that year I attached myself to a group of moneyed slackers helping a pal—a towheaded Adonis several years older than the rest of us—try to raise a sunken 1912 schooner from the muck at the bottom of Huntington Harbor. When this adventure later attracted the notice of a *New York Times* stringer, he filed a report about a band of "idealistic" volunteers from a "think positive" generation. It was not clear then, or ever, what was to become of the schooner if our "think positive" posse succeeded in getting it to float, yet after many grimy weeks and "hours of tension," we did. At last, the sodden hulk reluctantly if "dramatically" broke free from the sucking embrace of the muddy bed and "slowly rose to the surface" amid shouts of jubilation. It was towed ashore, made fast to the dock at a commercial boatyard, where it attracted a degree of local attention before the diesel baling pumps gave out and the sorry old tub subsided again to the harbor bottom.

Fridays, a band of us cut school after homeroom and—crowded into a Volkswagen bug purloined from a friend's hippie divorcée mother—made a beeline for the East Village to score hash on St. Marks Place and smoke up until it was time to catch a concert at the Fillmore East, where phenomenal seats were provided for us by a classmate's dad, a record-industry honcho. Properly stoned, we glazed over as amoeba projections created by the Joshua Light Show blobbed and shifted and blurred across the stage backdrops, and watched performances by Cream and the Buddy Miles Express and the still relatively unknown Jimi Hendrix. I remember almost nothing about the music, or whether Hendrix set his guitar afire, though I do recall clearly that he wore a velvet jacket, a concho belt, skin-tight bell-bottoms, and a fedora it enraged him to lose when a crazed fan ran onstage and snatched it from his head, leaving him with a kind of pancaked Afro.

The acid we have already begun to drop is new enough on the market that it is measured and sold in microgram doses, or "mikes," most of it procured from a friend of my sister's, a spacey Joni Mitchell look-alike given to utterances like "I'm just a spirit having a mortal experience."

By now a shift was underway for me, something well beyond the reach-of-puberty cliché, as my awareness grew of how little purchase my parents had on what you might optimistically term the realities of my existence. I went to class and scored good grades but had already begun to absent myself, convinced, in a fervent, romantic teenage way, that I was armoring myself against my parents' negligence by imagining that, like the cat in Kipling's *Just So Stories,* I was setting out into the world on my "wild lone," knowing full well that was a fiction.

Yet this was the summer of 1967 and a lot of people I knew were striking out on the road to Colorado, the first in our group to go the spirit-having-a-mortal-experience girl and then, after her, a spoiled and pretty doctor's daughter with a lisp and a wardrobe of patchwork denim who strolled out of an eleventh-grade art class one morning, called her boyfriend from a pay phone by the principal's office, and instructed him to pick her up in his father's spare car at the edge of the parking lot.

The pair dropped the car off at his parents' house, stuffed clothes in a backpack, and, as casually as if they were going for coffee, started to thumb their way west (with a brief reverse halfway to Jericho Turnpike when they suddenly remembered they'd inadvertently left her dog behind). It was weeks before they returned to Huntington, dressed now in embroidered curly-fur Afghan coats that smelled of goat, making a convincing charade of reintegrating themselves into the student body and quickly setting up a thriving commerce in the acid scored on their adventure.

Theirs were the drugs I tripped on all summer the year I turned sixteen, supplemented by the occasional peyote button from a stash someone scored on a Navajo reservation. Once, a friend and I managed to gag down a package of morning glory seeds from Burpee—well aware that they came coated with a mild toxin to deter just such misuse—and then puked so violently it was not quite obvious to us whether we were hallucinating or dying. Stoned on one thing or another, my sister and I and our ragtag group began roving the North Shore in our parents' cars—from Cold Spring Harbor to Glen Cove—pilfering stuff so profligately that a girl in our group became expert enough to take orders.

We boosted sirloin steaks from King Kullen; vintage seal-fur coats from sleepy secondhand shops; rock-and-roll vinyl albums; ornate silver frames and bisque-head dolls from antiques stores; and, once, a six-foot-long library table that I brazenly heaved past the matronly cashiers at the Community Thrift Shop.

After a time, we expanded our scope and started creeping onto the grounds of the abandoned estates littering the Gold Coast of Long Island, vast Gatsbyesque piles erected in the early twentieth century and now shuttered or abandoned.

The most stupendous of these was an austere Georgian mansion commissioned by an heir to the Marshall Field department-store fortune and crowning a hilltop overlooking the Sound in a location the Matinecock people designated "place by a sharp rock." Set amid 1,400 mostly wooded acres, it was reachable across a narrow causeway with, on one side, emerald wetlands and a broad bay on the other. As was often the case with estates operated as small fiefdoms, this one was surrounded by dependencies, staff houses, and outbuildings. Also, like many of the others, it had been offloaded by the heirs and purchased by New York State for a pittance. At some point in the future it would be transformed into public parkland, but that time was still far off. For now it was vacant and remote, unguarded, a magical kingdom. And while we were just sensible enough not to invade the main house, we roamed at will through the polo stables, milking parlors, hen coops, and hoop houses and greenhouses and icehouses on our nocturnal excursions.

I think now how gorgeous night felt as we took the steep hill to the causeway in a friend's old Army jeep, shutting off headlights and engine to coast downhill in neutral, the only sounds the whisper of rubber on pavement and wind through the open windows. It felt to us, in our tripped-out state, as though we were barreling through an eternally green tunnel, the tube of a time-bending wave, with the distant garland of Connecticut shorefront lights ahead of us and the prospect of climbing a vast copper beech tree whose vaulting canopy had become our unofficial trip-house.

If no memory of transformed consciousness survives from those brief hallucinogenic years—no radical visions or revelations—it is clear at least that we were going to some lengths to attract the attention and, by inference, love of our self-absorbed and otherwise distracted parents. Once, after spending a night on a friend's roof blasted on psilocybin, mesmerized by a summer storm etching the sky with lightning, I slumped home in the morning to find my enraged father awake and waiting. Somehow it had not occurred to me that my absence had even been noted. Thus I was as much startled as truly hurt when he threw me to the floor and trounced me.

Later in that same that week I returned to the beech tree with my friend Norah, so stoned at the time she saw pretty patterns in the tie-dye bruises around my shiner and linked them, in her mind's eye, to the kaleidoscopic light filtering through the branches. "I wish you could see what I see," Norah said in her dreamy fashion, and I did have that wish.

Then, as a coda, she added: "Isn't life deluxe?"

⚬ ⚬ ⚬

BY DECEMBER of 1968, we were in Acapulco. This was what we'd do at Christmas: with bags prepacked, we opened presents first thing and then left immediately for the airport. One year the trip was to Antigua, another year to Martinique. Hawaiian Surf had been prospering across the border so a family trip to Mexico could probably be sold to the accountant as a tax-deductible business expense. Our storied hotel was built on a cliff edge where, at timed intervals, divers plunged from a ledge into tidal pools 135 feet below. This scarifying spectacle, fascinating when seen once from the vantage of a hotel pool deck, did not reward repeat viewings. Or that, anyway, was the view of one spoiled sixteen-year-old hippie.

After a day of boredom I drifted off to the hotel gift shop, gliding in from the tropical heat to an enveloping rush of refrigerated air. Stocking the display shelves was the usual high-end souvenir junk: stone replicas of the Aztec calendar, silver cigarette boxes inset with tiles of abalone, dolphin-shaped bottle openers, and a book selection chosen by someone with unexpectedly subversive literary tastes. How otherwise to account for a gift shop in a luxury hotel at a high-end Mexican beach resort selling paperback copies of *Psychopathia Sexualis,* or Tennessee Williams's raunchy short-story collection *Hard Candy,* or a selection of the hothouse literary homoerotica of James Purdy? None of it is exactly beach reading. After shuffling around for a while with an eye on a snoopy salesclerk, I coolly lifted the von Krafft-Ebing from the rack and slipped it into my beach bag and then spent what remained of the holiday squirreled away in a shady corner poolside, ostentatiously ignoring my parents, siblings, and the storied cliff divers while reading up on "antipathetic" instincts that seemed to describe a lot of feelings I'd experienced but did not yet understand.

On another holiday, in another season of that same year, we flew to the French West Indies, a trip for which we kitted ourselves out beforehand at Brooks Brothers and Barneys with new dresses, new blazers, new silk repp ties. The resort's bookstore stocked *Réalités,* a French "journal of culture." This time I bought my reading material, then slumped around from one chaise to another on the white sand, idly flipping magazine pages until I got so bored by pictorials of Kyoto's geishas, the aged Matisse cutting paper collages, and Bardot sunning topless on the Riviera that I took it into my head to go horseback riding.

Though this was not an activity heavily promoted by the resort, there were some nags tethered beneath the sea grapes just outside the porte cochere. An attendant went off to tack one up and walk it to the hotel forecourt, where he handed me the reins and then slumped away wordless. When I think back on this day from the perspective of the skilled rider I will later train hard to become, it is clear that what followed could have been predicted. While it is true that the business part of a horse's brain is infamously the size of a walnut, the horse has not been born that cannot figure out how to get a monkey off its back.

Horses read you, and this one had my number before we'd trotted out the driveway, headed in the direction of a sand path running parallel to the beach. Having fudged my skills in the first place, I tried to make it look to a passerby as though the route decision were my choice, that I knew how to use the steering wheel and where to find the brakes. We moseyed along like this for a time at a jerky half-trot until, suddenly confident, I decided to take the speed up a notch with a mild kick to the horse's flanks. It was at this point that the scruffy gray gelding did what rank horses invariably do in these circumstances. He pinned back his ears and picked up pace, first to a canter and then an easygoing gallop that very quickly geared up to train-wreck velocity. Suddenly we were flying through a landscape blurred into streaks of green foliage and aqua water, my ears and the backs of my eyes pounding with blood.

The more I hauled on the reins, the more the horse set his teeth against the bit, racing first toward the water, where I briefly believed I might be able to leap off the saddle, then reversing course and making straight for a grove.

The tree branch came up so fast I was barely aware of raising my arm to shield my face. I was mounted and then I was sprawling in brush. Checking around me, I spotted the skull-and-bones warning wrapped around a caustic manchineel tree, relieved that I'd crashed into a sea grape instead, then I staggered to my feet and noticed that my right elbow jutted out at an unnatural angle. With the joint cradled in the palm of my good hand, I stumbled the mile or so back to the hotel, shimmied painfully over a perimeter wall, and, climbing the broad stair to the front desk, presented myself at reception, where a clerk looked up and dully said, *"Oui, monsieur?"*

Roughly about now my parents were enjoying a post-prandial cocktail beneath a fringed poolside umbrella. In another twenty-four hours we would all have boarded a chartered flight to Antigua, and from there a commercial one home for the emergency surgery to save the use of my arm. A French ER doctor encased the arm in a heavy plaster cast. An amiable dentist met on the beach produced a supply of painkillers from his travel medicine bag. That night, my brother and sisters and I stayed back in our suite, ordering up extravagant room-service offerings like mock turtle soup and foie gras, the soup poured down the toilet uneaten, the foie gras pushed out into the hall on its tray. We ordered again, this time club sandwiches and Cokes.

Our parents, in the meantime, had gone off to dinner at the hotel's formal restaurant. And in the memory I hold from that evening my dad looked uncommonly handsome in his navy-blue sport coat, and my mother's deep tan was set off by a pale ivory tunic from Nina Ricci. The scent of her fragrance—a custom lab blend from Givaudan labeled 5093J—drifted in the air as he placed his hand in the small of her back to guide her through the doorway. She assured me as they left that all would be fine. And, after all, how could they have thought otherwise?

They were still then golden young people, just past the midpoint of their thirties, and more than a little drunk on their unexpected good fortune. Fortified by a seemingly invincible glamour, they had somehow failed to envision situations in which things did not work out. Because they believed this we also did, a conviction that carried me along until at last I saw that what I had mistaken for confidence was in fact bravado, the emotional tool of children. By the time I came to this realization, my father was effectively a ruined man, my mother dead, Laura a convicted felon, my two other siblings scattered, and our house in cinders.

That was all far in the future. In the year I'm describing, the summer of Woodstock, Laura and her misfit crew will drive a borrowed VW van north to Max Yasgur's farm, whether making it or not I can't say for sure, and I will earn my first real paycheck. Before then my work experience had been confined to crackbrained schemes of my dad's to get his longhair son to trade the Landlubber jeans and fringed suede hippie moccasins for blazers and khakis, man up as an apprentice on a clam boat in the Great South Bay, and cast plaster tiki totems to be used by Hawaiian Surf vendors as novelty endcap displays.

Eventually, I struck out on my own and found an ad in the local Pennysaver. The job was for a part-timer at a record-pressing factory in Huntington Station, no job description detailed and none required, because the job was to stand robotically for hours feeding 45-rpm vinyl records from a conveyor belt to the machine that punched holes in their centers.

Before I took the job at Golden Crest Records, it had not occurred to me that vinyl records came without holes in the first place, like bagels or donuts, or to wonder why seven-inch singles had larger holes than those in 33-rpm albums. (It was to keep the smaller discs from going out of true in jukeboxes, as I learned, because discs whirred up to playing speed so fast in those things that the vinyl tended to torque and wobble.) I'd always assumed the process was automated, which turned out to be half-true, and that little human effort was involved, which was not. And I was wholly unaware of the history of Golden Crest Records, which, as I also learned, had for years been pressing rock and roll, doo-wop, classical music, chamber music, and jazz discs as a subcontractor for labels like Paramount, United Artists, Atlantic, and others.

The mechanics behind making the Top 40 hits that ruled the airwaves took place in this squat facility on Broadway near the tracks of the Long Island Rail Road in Huntington Station. Even if you were not stoned a lot of the time, as I was, a job like that had its perils. Since the discs flowed in an unending stream, both dexterity and concentration were required to grab them quickly, centering each between a pair of guide bumpers before a razor-sharp hydraulic hole punch whooshed down with a hungry pneumatic thud. Grab, feed, and release was the sequence, and the working rhythm was so dully hypnotic it was easy to slack off and carelessly lose a fingertip.

Once the shiny black vinyl discs were perforated and returned to the belt, they flowed to another set of workers who encased them in shiny paper sleeves. My coworkers were almost uniformly older than I was, female and black, and their detachment was impressive as they performed the soul-deadening work of sliding records into sleeves and sleeves into twelve-count holders and holders into hard-sided shipping boxes. While at first this was puzzling to me, eventually it resolved itself into lessons on both the conditions of acceptance and the dignity of honest work. In this way, Golden Crest Records became more than just the backdrop to one purgatorial summer: it was a master class on what it means to hang on to whatever it is you know to be your core.

The work the women on my shift did as they pressed and packaged Top 40 hits they'd never listened to was mechanical and mindless. That did not make them robots. The minute break time rolled around, the cramped little lunchroom— with its chipped steel lockers and wire-mesh windows, its two hardwood benches pulled up to a folding table—filled with the smells of cold fried chicken and wax-wrapped bologna on white bread and the racket of gossip, while Motown hits blasted from somebody's little Sony transistor.

Of all the workers, only one was about my age, a plump sweetheart with a pageboy haircut she processed to silken straightness, pulling a hot comb through it each morning, setting it every evening in foam rollers. The humidity in the un-air-conditioned plant obliged her to wear a scarf knotted tight to preserve the do, a kerchief that exposed just the nape of her neck and a fringe of tight curls at the nape she called her "kitchen." The factory floor was a fashion runway to her; no way would she appear looking anything less than her best.

L'Wraine was my friend there. Drawn to each other by age more than anything, we in no time began hanging out in the break room and then in an alley adjacent to the truck bay, where L'Wraine brought along her portable GE clamshell record player. Creamsicle-like in orange and beige, it had a hinged lid, a tote handle, a swiveling tonearm, and an integral speaker wedged under a grille. L'Wraine was a Virgo, as she frequently reminded me, her way of explaining the fastidious care she took of her person and possessions, her habit of blowing dust from the tip of a needle before dropping it on a record, and the reason she methodically sorted her 45s in a hard-sided cloth-covered tote, using alphabetical tabs on manila dividers to segregate the Ray Charles records from the Aretha Franklin and the Aretha from Wilson Pickett and Wilson from the Zombies discs, the Zombies being her sole concession to the white-boy bands of the British invasion. The Stones were cute, in a sleazy way, L'Wraine said, but they were imitators, whereas if you understood black music then you knew right away that the rising bass line and Colin Blunstone's breathy falsetto on "Time of the Season" had soul.

Ever since childhood, black music had been the aural backdrop of my life, at first in the form of calypso tunes my parents played but also with the Mahalia Jackson gospel my otherwise straitlaced grandmother blasted out from her stereophonic record cabinet as she prepared the two of us Saturday lunch. Black music was not called that at the time, of course; well into the sixties, it was labeled "race music" and stocked in segregated sections at the back of record stores, well away from the many musical genres it "inspired" (in the decades before that, RCA Records further drew the distinction by pressing blues and R&B records on orange vinyl), often enough in a merchandising ghetto where world-music obscurities like Indian sitar and Japanese koto were also exiled.

It was not that I disliked white bands or rock music; my first record had been a single of "Over Under Sideways Down" by the Yardbirds, shoplifted from a glass-fronted cabinet at F. W. Woolworth and used as a foundational entry in my teenage listening résumé. Holed up in my room, I blasted mostly Cream and Hendrix and Janis Joplin and Dr. John the Night Tripper and the Mothers of Invention and, sometimes, winsome English folk groups like the Incredible String Band, along with the occasional novelty acts like Sam the Sham & the Pharaohs. Through L'Wraine my listening tastes rapidly began to broaden.

Out in the alley she flipped through her file box, deliberating over discs before pulling out "Tighten Up" by Archie Bell & the Drells, gentling the needle onto the record, scrounging a roach from her handbag, then lighting it up and offering me a toke. In our fifteen-minute breaks, L'Wraine could manage to get us both mildly stoned, or anyway high enough to dance a bit. "No white-people moves" was her mantra, and what she meant was no expressive hippie flailing. L'Wraine showed me how to keep movement tight, the center of gravity low, and, without precisely intending to do so, she also instructed me in something subtler and finer: how to use dance to transport you from wherever you happened to find yourself. "Didn't you know that everything you learn, and everything you suffer, will come in useful at some time in your life?" a character asks somewhere in a Penelope Fitzgerald novel, and this lesson L'Wraine also taught me in that graveled truck bay on those hot summer afternoons.

By the time I figured this out, Hawaiian Surf would be

long gone; the house reduced to rubble; my father and kid brother moving from one cheap motel to another along Jericho Turnpike, what remained of their worldly possessions piled in the back of the car. My younger sister, Dana, would have fled to the West Coast, on a scholarship to a university she chose because it was in the farthest place in the contiguous forty-eight states she could get from the rest of us. And Laura's whereabouts would be a complete a mystery to me, although every so often in the years ahead the FBI would call me in for an update. My mother would be dead.

Like many vanishings in my life then and thereafter, my mother's had the atmosphere of a stage illusion, a disappearing trick. Her death came quickly in 1975, the year that *Jaws* debuted in theaters, the summer when John Williams's panic-inducing suspense music was inescapable on TV, that ominous movie trailer droning about "a creature alive today who has survived millions of years of evolution without change, without passion, and without logic." The mindless killing machine in the film, the one that would attack and devour anything, was a shark. But the indifferent God who created that particular "devil and gave him jaws" was also the author of incurable cancer. And I thought about him and his perverse sense of humor when a physician whispered to my dad that the pancreatic tumor that came out of nowhere to kill his wife was statistically more common among heavy-smoking black road workers in their sixties than forty-two-year-old Caucasian women.

There was a moment, of the kind that contains eternities, when in late June my mother lifted her blouse and asked me to feel a hard node in her midriff. "What do you think?" she asked me. Very soon thereafter came another such moment when, as we drove through the green tunnel of Route 25A to the North Shore Medical Center for testing we already knew to be futile, I found myself coldly doing the math. A doctor had already informed my father, in secret, that my mother might have as little as eight weeks left. By my calculation, she had already used up half her remaining time.

Somewhere I have another photo salvaged from the fire, this one taken on the broad veranda of an inn on Block Island where, with one last grand gesture and on our final family trip, my dad took his children after their mother was laid in the ground. Never again would we all be together in this way, but I could not know that then. And while I also don't recall the snapshot's whereabouts anymore, my memory is clear of how the light in the photo was suffused with a purity particular to New England skies, and how tanned and open were the young faces of these people so physically alike, with their long limbs and long noses, their deep-set questioning eyes, yet so obviously alone and moated by individual griefs. In the photograph as I remember it, none of us is hugging or touching, and no single gaze is focused on the camera lens. Together in that place for what will turn out to be the last time in our lives, we seem as remote from one another as strangers on a train or else, perhaps, like fugitives, each one looking for some way out.

o o o

THAT WAS IN AUGUST of 1975. I was not yet twenty-three. I was living at the time in the Bronx, jobless, and with a friend cohort composed primarily of people who thought nothing was more logical or essential than altering your name or biography or gender affiliation. On the magical stage set of a broken-down city, these people—my friends, my dramatis personae—costumed themselves in an array of improvised and constantly mutating identities, revising them as needed, shedding them at whim.

In the small crowd I ran with were two male roommates I would never know by any other names than Cookie and Kitty. There was a rubber-mouthed redheaded former child actor nicknamed Howdy Doody after the television marionette. There was Ray Johnson, the founder of the New York Correspondence School, who signed his relentless mail-art pieces using, among other aliases, the name Cora Spondant. There were also, peripherally, the omnipresent drag queens of the Warhol Factory, people I encountered often enough because someone knew someone who had shared drugs with or had sex with someone else, usually the diminutive blond horndog actor Eric Emerson.

In the small overlapping circles that constituted the downtown of that moment, the place where you were consistently likely to bump into the Warhol queens or most anyone else was a hole-in-the-wall on East Tenth Street that would today be categorized as a "vintage" clothing store but was really a ragpicker's joint. The place was called Bogie's. A beefy and disheveled Hungarian immigrant named Bogenstein owned it.

Ragpickers once abounded on the streets of New York, hauling their grubby two-wheeled carts, scavenging for cloth or paper to turn into cardboard, glass to melt down and reuse, and even, by legend, stray cats and dogs to skin for their pelts. The definition of a ragpicker as "one who makes a living by rummaging through refuse in the streets to collect material for salvage" applied equally to some of the types I knew then—although *"chiffoniers,"* the French term for rag trad-ers, better suits the flamboyant drag characters you spotted at Bogie's. The secret of the place was passed to me by a fireplug of a woman who styled herself Andrea Lucidity, her name deriving from a chichi Upper East Side boutique that sold ice buckets, phone caddies, wheeled television trays, and other household objects molded from translucent plastic. "Bogie's, you have to see it, go soon," Andrea Lucidity said.

And, as it happened, you did have to see Bogie's to get an accurate snapshot of the downtown of that moment because it was there, in a storefront off Second Avenue, that many scavenged the tatty raiment they then used to costume them-selves for performances staged as part of an ongoing personal theater, spectacles that occurred all the time on the streets of Manhattan. When I recall the people I knew then, I think of them as vedettes, stars in movies shot without benefit of cameras, or in improvised stage plays with no dialogue. They certainly thought of themselves that way. And they viewed as their public the rest of the population, tolerant New Yorkers who must have had no clue what to make of these apparitions, embodiments of Pessoa's observation that masquerade dis-closes the reality of souls.

What, I would be curious to know, could a regular Joe have thought when Howdy Doody vamped along dressed as though he had raided MGM's wardrobe department, sauntering arm in arm with another tatty queen gotten up in stuff unearthed from Bogie's bales and bins? Wherever they came from, the pickings at Bogie's were epic—slatternly housedresses from the thirties, spiky monkey-fur chubby jacket from the forties, velvet evening dresses, satin blazers with pagoda shoulders, twelve-button sailor pants with flap flies, and surplus M-1965 field coats fresh from the Vietnam War.

Tuesdays were delivery day, when Bogie razored open his fresh bales of old rags. And rummaging through the bins then you often found yourself scrabbling for treasures alongside Holly Woodlawn, not yet a Warhol star though well established as a local character and garrulous speed ranter, usually smelling like a goat. Holly would eventually be immortalized as a transgender actress, a one-time hooker who will live as long as anyone still plays "Walk on the Wild Side," Lou Reed's idealized ode to a group of bohemian characters Reed had, in point of fact, yet to meet when he wrote it.

In the twenty-first century we no longer use deadnames for transgender people, but in 1975, Holly was still also Harold Danhakl, an antic Puerto Rican queen who claimed to have arrived at her drag moniker by mashing up the adopted name of Truman Capote's most celebrated creation (Holly Golightly's alias was, of course, itself an invention) with something she'd caught in an *I Love Lucy* episode. In later decades Holly tweaked the legend and said she was descended from the founders of Woodlawn Cemetery in the Bronx. That there never was any such family somehow made it even better, since, after all, the family of camp was Holly's true lineage.

Like a lot of the other drag queens running around downtown Manhattan, Holly brought a febrile conviction to her everyday self-inventions and was never under any obligation to play the virtuous good girl. In her ongoing impersonation of some imaginary movie actress of the thirties she was a faded film goddess whose hand-to-mouth existence resulted from some unfortunate cosmic misalignment. "Look at me, honey," Holly said one day as she tugged a dress from under a heap at Bogie's. "I'm a star! I should be in movies! Instead, I'm reduced to selling my pussy in the street and I don't even have one."

Later on Andy Warhol would accurately note in his memoir *Popism* that most of the drag queens at that point were still hanging around "where they'd always hung around—on the fringes . . . sticking to their own circles—outcasts with bad teeth and body odor and cheap makeup." Bogie's was that sort of outcast hangout, a rathole but with its own kind of charm. After all, you might bump into Jackie Curtis (she lived around the corner on Second Avenue near Slugger Ann's, a bar owned by her grandmother Ann Uglialoro) or a doughy Off-Broadway "actress" who called herself Sweet Lips after her Tennessee birthplace, or else a willowy Garbo look-alike who went by the name of Sylva Thinn. Occasionally, even Candy Darling turned up.

Candy at that point had only recently settled on the image of herself that hardened into legend, having tried on and discarded a variety of personas since little James Lawrence Slattery of Massapequa Park, Long Island, first transmogrified himself into Hope Slattery. Not necessarily in this sequence, she then became Hope Dahl and Candy Dahl and later Candy Cane—which is what she was calling herself when she still shared SRO lodgings on West Eighth Street with a pock-marked transvestite sex worker called Porky—before settling on Candy Darling, a name that, it goes without saying, has a ring of the inevitable.

Decades on from this moment, I would find myself racing around New Delhi in a white Ambassador taxi with a novelist friend, a new pal with a Pop pseudonym he'd swapped out for his prosaic given name and that worked fine in his fringe downtown milieu, but much less well in the elevated literary circles where he rightly belonged. We were in India on separate magazine assignments, he in pursuit of an interview with an infamous, and notoriously sexy, mass murderer being held at Tihar Jail, and me on some story in no way worth remembering. Neither of us, in the end, produced whatever we'd been sent to write, though we made the most of our expense-account jaunt in what was still—in the days before the Indian economy was liberalized—an anachronistic capital city, with the drowsy genteel feel of Kennedy-era Washington. Talky and brilliant, a phenomenal mimic and epic drinker, my new friend was already tipsy by early afternoon as the two of us headed to South Delhi to view the Qutb Minar and afterward an abandoned sixteenth-century mosque and tomb consecrated to a Sufi saint and his male lover.

The marble mosque was poetic and spooky, buried in scrub forest and spattered with bat guano. Huge pendant wasp nests hung in the arches of screened marble windows. I had been reading a collection of Isak Dinesen essays and mentioned to my friend the Danish writer's insistence on having a personal motto.

"Well, Candy always did," my friend drawled, pulling hard on a Marlboro, exhaling the smoke through his nose.

Candy, in fact, was an inveterate self-improver who, right up to her death, logged lists and slogans and fortune-cookie adages and recorded her ever-changing mottos in a diary that would eventually be published in a facsimile edition, bound in pink vinyl and fastened with a "gold" lock and miniature key.

"Do you remember it?" my pal asked, and for the sheer pleasure of hearing his Candy imitation I pretended I did not. I knew already from mutual friends that better even than his impressions of Nico or his version of Dory Previn singing "Beware of Young Girls" was his take on Candy uttering almost anything, especially when she used the nasal intonations of Kim Novak playing Madge Owens in *Picnic*.

As the Sikh cabbie careered through a roundabout, overtaking a camel cart and a freight truck, my friend shut his eyes as if in a trance: "Good, good, good, better, better, better, best, best, best you can be," he purred in a perfect imitation of Candy's chloroformed purr. "Real, real, real," he went on. "Very real."

And that is the voice I hear whenever I recall a favorite Candy story, one she repeated about herself so often that you had to wonder how much of it was true.

In it, Candy had found herself strolling down a sidewalk one midwinter evening past the Triangle Civic Improvement Association, a Mafia "social club" on Sullivan Street. The place was the standard mob hangout from the period, pure Scorsese cliché: a street-level storefront in a redbrick tenement, a lace-curtained front door set between bow windows framed in peeling cast iron. As Candy painted the picture, you could easily envision the shelf in the window with a dusty statue of the Virgin and a prehistoric snake plant bursting its pot.

It was from just such a place that mobsters like Vincent "The Chin" Gigante ran the Genovese crime family empire: bookmaking, loan-sharking, shipping, trucking, construction, protection, heroin distribution, trash removal, and murder-for-hire. Though Gigante was a cunning goon who once had a rival bludgeoned to death with the flat of a shovel, he shambled about the streets of Little Italy dressed in shower shoes and a belted bathrobe, disguising himself as a harmless half-wit.

Dusk had fallen, as Candy told the story, and there was a light dusting of snow on the ground. Somehow, walking north along Sullivan Street as she nervously worried the cap on a speed-rotted front tooth with her tongue, she inadvertently flicked the thing out of her mouth. What was there for a nearsighted girl to do, was how Candy put it, except knock on the door of the social club?

"I've lost my pearl earring," said Candy. "Could you gentlemen help me find it?"

And, in her account, one or maybe several of the men inside grabbed flashlights, scanning the sidewalk to assist a pretty lady who, by this time of day, had usually begun to develop a five-o'clock shadow. Candy herself saw the cap first, its cheap enamel standing out whiter than the snow around it, quickly scooping it up to snap back onto the stump of her tooth. Pressing her fingers to her lips, she then blew her heroes a kiss before skittering away in her unseasonal sueded fuck-me pumps.

"It's such a pleasure," Candy said, "to know that there are still real men in the world."

That was how Candy told it, and it never occurred to me

at the time to question whether this scenario occurred. What mattered was that it could have. Or, rather, it had to have happened because that was the imaginative, cinematic way in which people like Candy Darling experienced themselves in the specific New York I am describing, at a time when it was not at all unusual for people to shop around for the reality best suited to whatever story they happened to be telling themselves at the time.

When I first heard Candy relate that story, I was twenty years old, spottily employed and scantily educated, having limped out of high school barely bothering to collect a diploma. I had audited some drawing and painting classes at Parsons School of Design and had no coherent career plan. My part-time day job was couriering actual moneybags for a Lebanese bank with headquarters across the street from the New York Public Library. If I was drawn to people like Candy, it was because I shared her desire to metamorphose, without knowing into quite what. This was not a matter of gender since I was comfortable with the one I conformed to genitally and had little interest in drag—except insofar as I recognized the hippie garb I was still wearing from high school as a form of costume, a camouflage of use to the people who employed me since it was clear no bandit in his right mind would think to stick up a longhair in a battered leather bomber jacket on a city bus. Never mind that I had tens of thousands of dollars in foreign currency in a canvas sack wedged between my feet.

That job was part-time. I worked from eleven until the bank closed at three, and afterward raced across town to Murray Hill to model for an illustrator who drew the menswear advertisements for important haberdasheries. My qualifications for the job amounted to little more than being tall and skinny enough to fit sample sizes.

It didn't matter if the trousers were too short. She'd draw them the right length. It was irrelevant that my shoulder-length hair was a far cry from the look of the preppies she sketched in their seersucker suits, their patchwork madras blazers, their heathery tweeds. She used her imagination to alter the details. Overall I made a superior stick figure, being able to hold poses against a length of seamless paper for long stretches of time, sometimes until my hands and feet went numb.

The modeling was a good gig. It paid better than being a messenger and, between the two jobs, I was able to cover my half of the rent on a Bronx apartment I'd begun to share with an artist friend, Paula Hyman, one among a gang of fashion-school types encountered at Parsons, a posse that also included a young fashion-illustration student from Queens named Steven Meisel and his closest friend, Anna Sui, a budding designer from the suburbs of Detroit.

I—perhaps more than anyone in this group—was in what I now think of as a dumb thrall to the city. It helped that in many ways the Manhattan of the 1970s was still an anachronistic and theatrical metropolis little changed from that featured in the prologue to *Million Dollar Movie,* a recurring oldies feature we watched religiously on television when we were young.

In the montage that opens the show, silhouetted night shots of behemoth Checker cabs alternate with flashes of rain-

Paula Hyman, Lloyd Neck, 1971

slicked avenues, the neon of Times Square blurring into shots of the Plaza Hotel or the gorgeously jetting fountains at Lincoln Center, all of it backed incongruously by Max Steiner's lush orchestral "Tara's Theme" from *Gone with the Wind*.

Even as late as the seventies, the visual textures of Manhattan remained shaped by the landmarks and folkways of a much earlier era. All this will change substantially in my lifetime, hundred-story residential towers defacing the skyline and casting sinister shadows across Central Park. But at the time I'm describing, the midtown skyline was still shaped by the elegant Art Deco ziggurats of the Chrysler Building and the spire of the Empire State Building, and throughout Manhattan there survived still a congeries of ethnic enclaves, first established as ghettos, hanging on as seemingly imperishable Old Country holdouts of Hungary or Poland or Ukraine or Germany.

Certain of the IND subway cars retained the stiff wicker seats of the 1930s and, at Radio City Music Hall, the Rockettes kicked in eternal unison as a feature of variety shows whose roots were in vaudeville. The burger joint where a fictitious Holly Golightly played bagman for the mobster Sally Tomato in *Breakfast at Tiffany's* was very much a real place, one where it was not unknown to find oneself at the counter next to Jacqueline Kennedy Onassis, like you, chowing down on a fifty-cent burger topped with house-made Hamburger Heaven relish spooned from a chrome-lidded jar. Food was astoundingly cheap in a city where at the Woolworth's counter a tuna-salad-stuffed tomato with saltines and a Coca-Cola could still be bought for seventy cents.

Some days, between messenger runs, I grabbed a skinny twenty-five-cent sandwich of cream cheese on date-nut at Chock Full o' Nuts. That generally held me until dinner. When there was time, I would occasionally drop into the cavernous Horn & Hardart automat with its plate-glass windows facing onto West Fifty-Seventh Street for a slice of apple pie dispensed from behind a glass door. The delight of the place was equally the delicious pie itself (the vast central automat canteen was just blocks away) and the magic of inserting a cashier-dispensed token in a slot and then lifting open a small window to retrieve your food.

While by now the place had long since lost its original luster as a bright and affordable working-class lunch spot, it was packed at every hour, often enough with lonesome souls lost in impenetrable solitude. Some but not all were homeless people, nursing dime coffees for hours from their viewing seats on the passing parade. On one windy afternoon once, I ducked into the automat and caught sight of the silent-film star Lillian Gish, wizened and rouged and teetering along the sidewalk outside. Even swaddled in a fur coat, she seemed weightless as a hankie, as though one blast off the river might blow her away, still an orphan of the storm.

It was another curious feature of this time-arrested moment in the history of the city how many of the biggest Hollywood stars, now aged and largely abandoned by the industry, had established a beachhead in Manhattan, "cut off like people on a desert island," as the film historian Robert Osborne would later observe. "Nobody gave a damn about Hedy Lamarr back then," Osborne added, though this was not entirely so.

Andy Warhol, for one, stalked and collected stars he'd idolized in his hardscrabble Pittsburgh boyhood, once-beautiful has-beens like Joan Crawford, Paulette Goddard, Joan Bennett, and Merle Oberon. Warhol's original ploy was the fan note, a method he'd elaborate on by founding *InterView* (as it was then spelled) to gain access to people and parties and, eventually, clients for the commissioned portraits that were his bread and butter. With no inkling of how to achieve the success I longed for, in a pinching if inchoate way, I started writing mash notes to various people, my choices almost random, among them the screenwriter and novelist Anita Loos. True, her Lorelei Lee was and remains one of the great and certainly most underrated (though not by James Joyce or Edith Wharton) characters in twentieth-century literature, but *Gentlemen Prefer Blondes* had been written in 1925. I must have laid it on thick since a reply arrived quickly by mail, inviting me to tea.

Neetsie, as I was invited to call Miss Loos, dressed habitually in ensembles from Balenciaga, had her steel-gray hair cut in the pixie bangs of a schoolgirl, and concealed her shrewd ancient eyes behind saucer-size sunglasses that gave her the look of a quizzical bug. Tea, as I learned, was a tall-boy of gin nursed steadily in the plant-filled solarium of an immense apartment in the Briarcliffe on West Fifty-Seventh Street. There Miss Loos lived with a maid-companion who drifted in and out periodically, as if on cue, to refresh the tiny octogenarian's cocktail.

It is anyone's guess as to where I thought encounters like this might lead, but as a toehold along the path of a striver it then seemed sufficient, and the point is that Neetsie told good

Anita Loos, author of Gentlemen Prefer Blondes

stories. You did not have to know much or even care about the Golden Age of Hollywood to enjoy her tales of riding in Packard caravans from Los Angeles to William Randolph Hearst's castle, La Cuesta Encantada, on the newly constructed Pacific Coast Highway, or of the movie people she knew sneaking forbidden hooch onto the grounds. Neetsie regaled me with stories of Marion Davies, then she spoke of the endearingly drunken chatelaine of San Simeon secreting vodka bottles in eighteenth-century cachepots, of Paulette Goddard (born, as Neetsie liked to point out, Pauline Levy of Great Neck) hiding the emeralds Erich Maria Remarque gave her in Quaker Oats boxes. She spoke of Archibald Leach masterfully concealing a situationally adaptable sexuality behind the dream-factory mask of a persona called Cary Grant and, as Neetsie sipped iced gin and I nursed a warm Coke, my thoughts toggled by reflex to the freaks I had by then fallen in with, mostly the provisionally famous or the Warhol-adjacent.

Most of these were exotic characters who would almost uniformly die too young to benefit from their own burgeoning legends and who were never, anyway, destined for conventional success. And I traded Neetsie stories about them—about people like Sylva Thinn, the lunar drag beauty who slunk around town dressed in silk Sulka shirts scavenged from thrift stores, high-waisted trousers, scarred leather bombers, and a creased beret, always with a lighted Craven A in hand. Even then I didn't truly know Sylva as a boy or even as a dimensioned human being, so most of what I gleaned about this glamorous and inscrutable personage came decades afterward. In part this was because while so many of the garrulous drag queens were gaily self-mythologizing motormouthed speed freaks, Sylva was a sphynx.

Following a meteoric early orbit through the Factory firmament, a few Off-Broadway shows, some fashion shoots engineered by slumming *Vogue* editors, Sylva would soon decamp for her hometown of Athens, Georgia, and reclaim his childhood name and birth-assigned gender. As Jeremy Ayers, they went on to teach yoga, create an experimental gay salon, cowrite a song for R.E.M., and eventually become an Occupy Wall Street activist before dying at sixty-nine of a seizure.

Like many of the Warhol queens, Sylva achieved a kind of unlikely immortality, although not in the annals of downtown, or at least not directly. Somehow along the way Sylva befriended the musician Michael Stipe and when, in homage to R.E.M., a German entomologist and music fan offered to name a newly discovered species for the band, Stipe suggested instead that he name the ant for Sylva. Discovered in the Ecuadoran rain forest, the insect was called *Strumigenys ayersthey,* the binomial intentionally nonbinary. In a sense, like Sylva Thinn, it belonged to a taxonomical group with a single member.

Sylva quit New York forever for good around 1974. Before leaving town she and I and Richard Sohl (another Parsons pal who dropped out of art school to play piano in a band fronted by a then-unknown Patti Smith) decided one day, for no rational reason, to stalk Greta Garbo.

If anyone under Medicare age remembers Garbo, then they know the Garbo legend and the durable if questionable lore about her wanting to be alone. In truth she was a gregarious social being within certain rarefied circles, and a great walker in the city.

Friends from Parsons seemed to spot her all the time in the vicinity of the Campanile, her cooperative on a cul-de-sac at the foot of Fifty-Second Street or else around the corner of Fifty-Third Street and Third Avenue, where male hustlers lurked for johns, or else combing the plentiful and jumbled antiques shops all along First Avenue in the sixties. One morning, Sylva and Richard and I met at a coffee shop on First Avenue and, fanning out, formed a hopeful search party seeking a glimpse of our elusive quarry, agreeing to reconvene to trade notes in three hours.

That Garbo never materialized almost goes without saying. Yet, as I wandered the side streets of her native habitat, I happened upon something more compelling to me—a scene that, without my being aware of it, was a signpost toward what would eventually become my profession. It was a weird kind of episode, not all that uncommon at the time: two pigeon pirates scattered seeds on a stretch of sidewalk and stood back as more and more birds fluttered to the ground. By the time a decent flock was assembled and feeding, the two men had stationed themselves on the curb with a large throw net stretched between them. At some unseen signal they flung the net over the flock and swiftly pulled it taut, first pinning the birds to the ground, bundling them into a noisy mass of feathers and beaks and heaving their haul into the back of a parked panel van. Where they went then I did not know at the time; researching urban lore about pigeon pirates, I later learned that sometimes the birds were used as live bait at cockfights, sometimes as food for exotic reptiles, sometimes as shooting targets by out-of-state gun clubs, and occasionally—this must be apocryphal—as "squab" on the menus of fine French restaurants.

Baffling as the episode was, and easy enough to slough off in a city where the inexplicable is an everyday occurrence, it awakened something in me, returned me abruptly to a sense of the city I remembered from my earliest childhood years in the Bronx, when I was set free to wander our quiet Parkchester neighborhood with an improbable, now almost unimaginable, degree of freedom. It is not unique to my youth that I was caught up in the mystifying and thrilling workings of the world, my imagination during life's first years lighting up at every sight and sound; the novelty of adults hurtling slantwise past me on sidewalks; women chattering conspiratorially as they mobilized baby carriages the size of small cars; the cloying, addictive aroma of candy store shelves stocked with Pixy Stix, Razzles Fizzles, Necco Wafers, Bonomo Turkish Taffy, and chocolate-covered halvah. What was singularly mine, it seems, was a need to turn everything into a story.

Much later my fascination with the textures of things will occupy a lot of my working life as I spend years exploring aspects and corners of the metropolis few know and fewer still care to. Without yet understanding it, I had found in the pigeon rustlers elements of a subject—New York City itself—and, by way of it, a profession. At the time, of course, all of that remained well in the future.

Around then, although I had begun sketching out scripts for imaginary plays I fantasized staging Off-Off-Broadway, I had given little thought to writing as a career. Writing was not part of the plan because, if I am being truthful, there was no plan. Still, in most ways I was lucky to find myself in the New York of 1975, in a city navigating a dire fiscal crisis and at what I now see as a pivotal moment in the arc of its history. What I mean is that from the end of World War II until President Gerald Ford told New York to drop dead, the hardscape of the city remained in most ways static. While in the three decades that followed, that same city would be radically developed and altered, this was a fine time to be writing about the place, so much so that when I later collected for a book some of the hundreds of newspaper pieces I'd written, the title the publisher and I settled on was *In the Place to Be*. And, yes, it was that.

By the early nineties, I would have long since traded an existence that seemed random to the point of absurdity for a job and a craft and a paycheck and some measure of professional coherence. Never having set foot on a college campus, I was habitually surrounded by precociously overeducated and intellectually astute types who either generously or condescendingly made room for me and my ignorance of my chosen craft. And if I was not particularly inhibited by a lack of obvious work qualifications, I chalked it up to early lessons taught me by brilliant misfits whose gifts resisted pigeonholing—people like Jackie Curtis.

It is a frigid early-seventies afternoon, and I am perched on the edge of an unmade bed in Jackie's cluttered Second Avenue loft. Sun falls in pointed slabs through arched windows of a building, constructed in the Moorish revival style, that once housed a Yiddish theater and later morphed into an art-house multiplex. Playwright, poet, chanteuse, Warhol film star, gender renegade, and ubiquitous downtown presence, Jackie is racing around the loft shirtless and manic, waving a safety razor.

Half the torso of this reigning queen of Off-Off-Broadway—author of legendary downtown nonhits like *Vain Victory* and *Glamour, Glory and Gold: The Life and Legend of Nola Noonan: Goddess and Star*—is shaved smooth. The other remains densely furry. Thinking of her now, what Jackie resembled was in some sense a redheaded, speed-freak version of Ardhanarishvara, the twin-sexed Hindu avatar of Shiva. This was the Jackie of Alice Neel's portrait *Jackie Curtis as a Boy,* dual in nature, a winsome and insecure man who also happened to be a tough, protopunk female goddess given to wearing laddered fishnets, floozy frocks, and ankle-strap platforms.

"I'm not a boy, not a girl, not a faggot, not a drag queen, not a transsexual," as Jackie once said. "I'm just me, Jackie."

But Jackie, whatever she was, cannot focus, alternating distracted swipes at her remaining body hair with some rant or other, as last night's trick wanders about looking for a match to fire up a joint. Whether she was in makeup that day I don't recall, any more than I remember the precise reason I was there in the loft, although most likely it was because a nurse friend had invited me along with him to drop off some stolen Dexamyl, a wonder drug Smith, Kline & French marketed for depressed and *verbally inhibited* patients, italics mine. It was exciting to be there, thrilling to be in a room with this unfettered madcap being whose nearness to the Warhol Factory I hoped would rub off on me, along with her skill for writing hilarious, incoherently campy scripts.

"Cunt won't cast me in anything else," Jackie is saying, looking bemused with her clownishly arched eyebrows, though she clearly is not. Jackie is referring to Paul Morrissey, the director of the feminist satire *Women in Revolt,* which featured Jackie and Holly Woodlawn as radical women's libbers and Candy Darling typecast as a stuporously bored Upper East Side socialite.

"Cunt" and "twat" are all-purpose terms in Jackie's vocabulary, murmured as endearments, spat as maledictions although, alas, never spoken as anatomical descriptors of herself. It is Jackie, after all, who, when once asked what gift she would most like to have, replied: "The ability to give birth to a mynah bird, so my twat could talk."

Jackie's characteristic form of gab is like that, a free-associative flow of intellectual earnestness and amphetamine-fueled high faggotry. Crackling across the motherboard of Jackie's brain at any given time are innumerable cultural references, any of which lights up at random—acidulous, unashamedly whip-smart, and delivered in the rat-a-tat style of a Warner Bros. moll. Some part of me would like to be able to talk like that, to toss off stinging repartee. Yet I am shy and unconfident and through with drugs, having indulged so lavishly during what passed for my high school years that I've lost all taste for mind-altering anything.

And that turned out to be a stroke of dumb luck for me, since first the speed and then the other assorted drugs that worked as accelerants on people like Jackie also hastened them to seedy and predictable finales. Jackie is thirty-eight when she overdoses on heroin in 1985. By then Candy is long dead of the lymphoma that her friends persistently attributed to her lavish, unregulated misuse of bootlegged estrogen. Up to the end Jackie and Candy epitomized for me a yearning F. Scott Fitzgerald might have been referring to when he wrote that, for some, it is "always the becoming . . . never the being."

When I think of Jackie and Candy and those other pioneers now, with their smeared rouge and tinsel auras, I view them as progenitors of lineages, originators of all the drag begats. It would take time before academics formalized what Jackie and her nutty cohort instinctively knew about gender as performance. Yet even now those drag queens get too little credit for ideas that, as Paul Morrissey once remarked, they had in overflowing abundance. Consider the storied black-and-white portrait of Candy Darling on her deathbed, equal in power to any of the greatest portraits. In it, Candy—her beauty by then reduced to ethereal essence—reclines in her hospital bed at Columbia University Medical Center, platinum hair coiffed, fully made up, a rose on her pillow, a stylized spray of white chrysanthemums afloat behind her like the background in a Japanese woodblock. The image, staged in collaboration with photographer Peter Hujar, remains among his most celebrated and is also surely the one that safeguards a measure of immortality for Candy, capturing her seemingly unaltered by the inexorable processes of her own decay. For Candy that photograph was an apotheosis, a summary of her brief existence (she is twenty-nine when she dies).

"I will not cease to be myself for foolish people," Candy once confided to her diary. "For foolish people make harsh judgments on me. You must always be yourself, no matter what the price."

∘ ∘ ∘

WHAT IS EASY to forget now is that those Factory people were just one faction in the teeming microecology of downtown New York. There were many clans and I seemed for a while to float in and out of most. There was the Halston crowd of friends and rent boys and hangers-on and gorgeous young models and the amputees Halston occasionally hired to fulfill certain sexual needs, as well as the omnipresent Venezuelan artist and pest Victor Hugo. There was the joyous planetary system revolving around the light of Antonio Lopez, the Puerto Rican fashion illustrator of boundless generosity, to me and numberless others. There was the posse of male beauties scouted as models by the wiry Hungarian Zoltan "Zoli" Rendessy for his maverick agency, Zoli, men like Joe Macdonald and Kalani Durdan and Robert Yoh who would define masculine beauty for a generation. There was the Calvin Klein coterie of newly wealthy and empowered gay professionals with lives that centered around meat-rack summers at Fire Island Pines. There was a network of art types linked through the matrix of one brooding truculent and irresistible artist—that is, the photographer Peter Hujar. There were the cult deejays who had only recently begun to transform a hobby into a profession, hauling milk crates of prized vinyl discs from one obscure club to another, camp followers trailing behind.

One small group I fell in with for a time centered on a fashion illustrator I will call A., an unusual character, in my experience, for holding down a tenured job teaching at Parsons School of Design. The job was ideal for A. since it left him lots of free time to cruise department-store restrooms for sex, his favorite hunting ground being a men's bathroom near the housewares department on Bloomingdale's sixth floor. Between tricks, A. trawled Manhattan's countless thrift shops for stuff he arranged around him in a cramped rent-controlled tenement walk-up on East Fifty-Ninth Street, a fifth-floor dump with a water closet off the kitchen, an epic roach population, and, overall, the cloistered air of a tomb.

Entered through the kitchen, A.'s place was, even when I first met him, crammed to overflowing with bargain finds from his daily, sometimes hourly, shopping excursions. Silk scarves were flung in layers over antique lampshades. A brass bed doubling as a living room sofa was covered with so many quilts it resembled skeet-blanket mille-feuille. Rattan chairs were upholstered in 1930s bark cloth. Art Deco vases cluttered every horizontal surface. Fringed satin souvenir pillows commemorating visits to Niagara Falls or Coney Island or Winona, Minnesota, were piled all around. Beaded curtains hung from doorframes but the two tall windows facing onto the ramp of the Fifty-Ninth Street Bridge were left naked because A. liked the way car headlights strobed the place at night, flaring on barely demarcated zones for eating, fucking, and the bathing A. did none too often.

A.'s scavenging compulsion, it turned out, was a contagion; sooner or later, everyone in his orbit caught it. Each of us kept lists of special spots to hit, itineraries, carefully husbanded intelligence on when the new-old stock would circulate onto the floor at the Memorial Sloan Kettering Cancer Center or

the Arthritis Foundation thrift shops or else the cavernous
Everybody's Thrift Shop, to which A. made daily pilgrimages.
It was there that he snagged the hundreds of pastel Fiesta-
ware plates and jugs he collected, along with McCoy pottery
pitchers and blue-mirrored Moderne tables and hand-printed
chintzes in what the poet James Schuyler once characterized
as "East Fifties queen taste." Conjuring a mental image of
A. out shopping, I see a dowser with a string bag in the crook
of his elbow, a junk-store divinator magnetized by unseen
forces.

Seemingly no one could top A. for obsessive, maniacal
accretion, and gradually his living space became a trove
of whatever was his latest passion. Soon after discovering a
cookie jar in the shape of a stereotypical Southern "mammy,"
his apartment began to fill up with other examples in the
shapes of pigs or beehives or owls or pixies or tonsured monks
or mice or polar bears or circus horses. There was Popeye,
Bozo, and Snow White of the seven dwarfs. Eventually, A.'s
cookie jar collection would outstrip that of his principal rival,
Andy Warhol, although it would be Andy's hoard that fetched
staggering returns when 175 cookie jars of his were hammered
down for $247,830 at a posthumous Sotheby's sale.

By that time A. had long since moved on and turned instead
to that most macabre of collecting categories: dolls.

A., it now seems to me, was early to many trends, including a localized version of the gender-fuck dressing that the
Cockettes—the hippie queer San Francisco collective that
included the future disco star Sylvester—had already put into
play on the West Coast. Charles Ludlam and his Theatre of

the Ridiculous troupe also shamelessly vamped gender stereo-types, although with less glitter and seldom, if ever, offstage. Radically for the time, A. and his cohort ran around town attired in garb that cut across gender, class, and time, phenom-enal stuff from the men's and the women's sections, whether lawn boxer shorts from the 1930s, rayon housedresses from the 1950s, Gurkha shorts, or striped bib overalls to wear with ankle socks and alligator-skin platform shoes.

It says something about the laissez-faire atmosphere of seventies Manhattan that A.'s off-kilter getups aroused little controversy or even much notice, though he did tone things down for the classroom and when meeting with *Mademoiselle* editors to discuss drawing assignments. Whenever A. wasn't instructing "Introduction to Fashion Illustration" classes or shopping or fucking strangers, he directed self-scripted Super 8 films, financed on his salary, shoestring affairs that were visu-ally lavish if soundless, producing roughly one a month. His stars were pals and, on occasion, his students, and he treated them dictatorially, as if he were D. W. Griffith.

The casts ran to an assortment of gifted crazies—most, though not all, gay—who seem to have arrived in Manhattan in exile from Elsewhere, all intent on making it there because, in those benighted times, it was understood that there was little room in most small towns for people like them. In that crowd were Howdy Doody and those two antically bitchy window-dressers, Cookie and Kitty, and Richard H., an undertaker's son from western Pennsylvania with a lacerating tongue and an enormous penis (as he was quick to inform you).

Richard H. was first in the group to shave off his eyebrows, to wear satin for day, to clank around town with armloads of ivory bangles on his arms in imitation of the drug-addled 1930s heiress Nancy Cunard. Richard H.'s experimentation with punk dressing began years before Malcolm McLaren and Vivienne Westwood opened their London shops SEX and Seditionaries or, for that matter, before the term "punk" was coined. Nights, Richard H. would squat cross-legged on a mattress in his apartment, shredding his clothes, lopping off sleeves, excising collars, scissoring up inseams, suturing the varied elements together Frankenstein-style with safety pins. Part of this was creative expression and part a ploy to get himself fired from his job in the furniture department of Lord & Taylor for wearing inappropriate attire, unemployment benefits being roughly equivalent to an arts grant at a time when qualifying for welfare was like winning a MacArthur prize.

Most fragile and fascinating among A.'s ragtag followers was a man named Herman Costa, a tall creature who drew textile patterns for a living, wore a lavish Smith Bros. beard, and had the anomalous air of a wounded fawn. The vulnerability Herman exuded gave him an uncanny ability to take on the unlikeliest of roles. He played Marilyn Monroe in one film, for example, in full makeup and beard.

Whenever he was not at work or filming, Herman took to escaping to Woolworth's for the bargain sundaes, and to gossip with waitresses so accustomed to human oddities that they were unfazed when a hairy-chested man in a housedress and with glitter rouge spots on his cheeks ordered extra maraschino cherries for his banana split.

When he had finished, Herman inevitably headed for the

rear of the store and an alcove where the photo-booth device was installed. At first on occasion and then once weekly and finally every day, Herman took to sequestering himself in the booth, twirling the adjustable stool to accommodate his height, drawing the nubby wool half curtain shut, and plugging quarters into the machine. His project was self-portraiture, and he began with standard poses, the usual four shots of full face, profile, three-quarter view, and smile. Soon enough he tired of mugging for the camera and began to treat the booth as a studio for what he did not yet consider his art. "I started when everyone was growing their hair or shaving their heads," Herman said years later, referring to the daily record he made over more than a decade, a memoir told in images and, it goes without saying, an existential yelp.

One day it was woolly Herman, and the next, Herman in a cascading Jayne Mansfield wig, then Herman in a bald cap, staring with beady, mad Rasputin eyes. There was Herman in a fez, tiny spectacles, and a smock, late-period Matisse; and Herman scrunched on the stool like Quasimodo, his body distorted by the camera's inflexible lens. There was Herman back and front and, frame by frame, Herman's arm and leg and thigh and shoulder. It required careful timing to get the images right, so Herman took to rehearsing in the booth to save on quarters. Because there are no negatives, each photo-graphic strip was unique, each a "fine-grained and beautiful" black-and-white image that, as he suggested, was more poi-gnant for being created in this public and yet simultaneously private place that facilitated abandon. Who has ever failed to stick their tongue out in a photo booth?

Because there was a time lag while the images developed, Herman increasingly colonized the device and its little alcove, ramping up production by dragging props into the store from the apartment he had rented across the hall from A. Scrims; dolls, toys, rug fragments, mirrors, plants, and, occasionally, friends were spirited into Woolworth's. This went on for a surprisingly long while before the manager put a stop to it. By then Herman, who had begun to make a name for himself as a photo-booth auteur, was eventually assigned a dedicated machine at the headquarters of the Auto-Photo Company, which distributed them.

The Woolworth's booth returned to its primary use as a means for taking passport photos, and I soon lost contact with Herman and with most of that crowd, although only after filming one last movie with A. titled *Money in Egypt*. In it, Paula and I portrayed sex slaves kidnapped from a Riviera villa by the sleazeball Egyptian playboy King Farouk, and that is all I remember about the film or the other members of the cast. Most had by then begun to outgrow A. anyway, had shed their glad rags to seek straight jobs and embark on what would turn out to be surprisingly successful careers as photographers, designers, decorators, art directors, illustrators, and stylists. I was twenty-two when we made *Money in Egypt* and naturally still experienced myself as immortal. I mention this because any of us would have said you were crazy had you predicted that, with very few exceptions, each one of those people would be dead in barely more than a decade.

By then Paula and I were living in a five-room first-floor apartment in a largely Irish neighborhood in the north Bronx.

The area was far away from downtown and would never become cool. That didn't matter because even we could easily manage the $75 monthly rent. That part of the Bronx was then, as it remains, so sleepy and remote from Manhattan that we sometimes took to calling the place our country retreat.

It was a railroad-style apartment with two bedrooms facing the street and, across it, a hillside crested by a Catholic girls' school named for a virgin martyr. A paneled and painted living room separated the sleeping areas from the kitchen, a hallway, and a farther bedroom that faced onto the service yard. Here in what may once have been a nursery or a maid's room the childless landlord and his wife had operated a hobby ceramics business. Why anyone would squander a second of life making slip mold casts of Dürer's *Praying Hands* remains an enigma. Yet it was something they shared and, when the landlord's wife died, he shuttered the business and moved to Florida, subletting to us on condition that we leave the ceramic room in its pristine shrine state. So we kept the door shut on the tidily shelved Mayco molds frosted in kaolin dust, the two Cress and Evenheat kilns, the various shepherdesses and trolls and Christmas trees arrayed on steel standing shelves to await glaze-firing, as half-baked as the two of us.

By the bohemian standards of friends living in Bowery ratholes, our place was a palace: no stewbums nodding out in doorways, no junkies shooting up on the stairs. Naturally, we had to earn a living, so with few obviously marketable skills, I settled on making stuff, initially purses that were fancier versions of peasant market bags my hippie friends slung crossbody, deep oblong suede things with fringed flaps decorated with glass beads threaded onto each strand to form Navajo-blanket patterns. Once we'd decided to go into business, Paula and I began traipsing around Manhattan in search of the specialist suppliers that still existed in abundance. There was the guy in SoHo who sold split hides, pulled from stacks in a storefront on Lafayette Street that reeked of urea from tanning. There was a hole-punch place in the West Thirties run by a baby-faced Hasidic guy with flushed cheeks and tightly coiled *payes*. From him we learned of a bead place on Twenty-Ninth Street in what was still the Garment Center, and we splurged like idiots there on pounds of colored Czech beads that exhausted our savings. Having run low on cash, we shoplifted from Pearl Paint the heavy utility knives we needed and used what was left on an industrial-gauge hole punch with a spoked wheel. Then, on a trash-scavenged porcelain table in our Bronx kitchen, I drew out a proper paper pattern for the bags, transferred it to stiff manila sample paper, and lightly chalked out the segments on each hide, a jigsaw game to minimize waste before plunging knife blade into expensive suede.

The work was mind-numbing enough to induce concentration at the level of a trance state. Steadily for a week I pieced and marked, scored and cut, repeating the process until blisters came up in the web of flesh between palm and thumb. I punched holes through the segments to whipstitch them together, then cut fringe using a T square to steady the knife blade.

The design called for threading the fringes through a prepunched front panel, and marrying the elements left no room for error. While I labored to create this stuff, Paula got busy with a merchandising plan centered on canvasing the high-end specialty shops like Bonwit Teller, places that still held open-to-buy mornings once a week when indie vendors queued up to hawk their wares. It surprised me to learn, later, how many fashion designers had begun their careers this way, rolling racks of samples through midtown in the pre-dawn hours. We had no such ambitions, were not at all sure we could envision our funky hippie handbags—impractically deep, unlined, and with a single interior pocket—in establishments that featured doormen in pillbox hats and mirrored salons that sold "better" dresses, hats, and mink coats.

"Is this going to work?" I asked Paula, whose father manufactured coats and who had a good feel for the mystifying fashion world. Waving off my skepticism, she slung a bag across her torso to see how it worked with her outfit. "You'll see," she said, delighting in the noisy clacking sound the beads made as she twirled.

And she was right, as it happened: Henri Bendel immediately placed an order equal to our entire upfront outlay plus two months' overhead. Then a street-style photographer snapped Ali MacGraw wearing one of the bags, the picture was featured in the "People Are Talking About . . ." section of *Vogue,* and, ready or not, we were in business. From Paula's perspective it was bonanza time, yet—because a future in handbag design was not quite what I'd envisioned—I decided, almost as quickly as we'd started, to ditch the fringed hippie handbags after the first reorder. Then, of course, the money ran out and we were stuck, and so we went back into business, this time making novelty bracelets from thrift-shop-scavenged

mah-jongg tiles or colored plastic dice. Since we figured a business ought to have a letterhead, we named ourselves "Frying
Pan Ranch," after a name I'd overheard in some obscure thirties Western, and ordered printed invoice pads. Once again,
our designs, if they could be called that, took off and, following a *Women's Wear Daily* mention, Bendel's placed a second
order, for several hundred bracelets, a prospect more alarming
than exciting since there were ten dice to each bracelet and
these were drilled by hand in a cheapo vise that I had screwed
to a kitchen counter, then manually threaded onto elastic cord.

Once again, ambition petered out and I abandoned our
accessories business. Paula equably relinquished whatever
hopes she may have had for our shared enterprise and went
searching for temp work, and I briefly cadged a real job for
which I was outstandingly unequipped, as a night-shift bus-
boy at Mickey Ruskin's storied canteen, Max's Kansas City. I
stuck the job out long enough to get an unappetizing glimpse
of the famous back room, which to my eyes was less a bohemian paradise than a plywood-paneled high school cafete-
ria packed with freeloaders desperately sponging off Andy
Warhol. Semifamous people did sing for their supper, but it
was only interesting once to see sad, stoned Andrea Feldman
climbing atop a table to croon her rendition of the folk singer
Melanie's "What Have They Done to My Song Ma," with the
lyrics altered to "Look what they've done to my brain."

My stint at Max's was too brief for me to attract even the
slightest attention from anyone of importance, and certainly
not long enough for me to pick up any tricks of the restaurant trade. I was never sure whether to go backward through

the swinging service doors or kick them open as I hauled a tub full of food-encrusted dinner plates, or what to do when waitresses cheated the tip pool, and less still how to deflect the tantrummy rants of a manager who ducked constantly into a pay-phone booth to do coke bumps.

Part of my job was preparing the restaurant's signature dessert, an orb of vanilla ice cream rolled in coconut flakes. One evening, as I went to fix a customer's "Snowball," the aluminum scoop hit something hard in the commercial ice cream tub. Excavating around the obstruction I took to be frozen ice cream, I found instead the T-bone from a half-eaten steak. A waitress hustling past me to the ticket rail paused to ask what the problem was, and I stepped away from the top-loading Galaxy freezer and pointed toward the embedded leftover. How would you handle the situation, I asked. "Scoop around it," she said flatly as I untied my apron, threaded through the packed bar crowd, and walked out the front door.

That would be the pattern of my first years in New York, from roughly eighteen to twenty-three, when I toggled between harebrained entrepreneurial schemes, nothing jobs found on the moccasin telegraph of the disposable-worker gig economy, and a welter of unfocused creative pursuits. It was not, after all, the worst education. Everybody has read that Manhattan in the mid-1970s was a city on the skids; a thriving literary subgenre has grown up around the fact. Lucy Sante (then writing as Luc Sante in *Low Life*) was exaggerating, though not by a lot, in noting that "aside from the high-intensity blocks of Midtown and the financial district, the place seemed to be inhabited principally by slouchers and loungers, loose-joints vendors and teenage hustlers, panhandlers and site-specific drunks, persons whose fleabags put them out on the street at eight and only permitted reentry at six."

What is too little remarked on is how somnolent and dreamlike the city could be, how in many ways magical appeared this wrecked and depopulated metropolis, my classroom. Great swaths of the city were desolate. The triangle between Canal Street and the World Trade Center (not yet formalized as "Tribeca") was so hushed at night as to feel like the abandoned back end of some small town, a place where you could ride a bike down the middle of Hudson Street after dark. Everywhere you ventured were forgotten corners, hidden places; shoreline verges dense with reeds and cattails; abandoned piers; smutty aprons of beach lapped by an even dirtier Hudson; dead-end alleys; parks overgrown with sumac, ailanthus, and other opportunistic weed trees; labyrinthine railway tunnels that were the habitat of feral cats and bands of vagrants who, entering through a secret gate in an overpass off the West Side Highway, descended to honeycombed warrens of concrete niches furnished with castoffs and lighted by candles, a Neronian scene.

In blaring contrast to these shadowed places was the raunchy gaud of midtown, simultaneously bleak and gorgeous, washed in yellow light from the marquees of opulent movie palaces from the early part of the twentieth century, now decadent and seedy and relegated to playing soft-core triple bills or blaxploitation features like *Hell Up in Harlem* or zombie films like *Tombs of the Blind Dead*. Hookers—not yet professionally dignified as "sex workers"—worked the Eighth Avenue stroll in

Times Square clad in rabbit-fur jackets, crinkled vinyl boots, and satin hot pants. Their pimps operated from cheap rooms at the Hotel Carter or else Smith's bar, where in later years a cop on a meal break would kill himself at a table, just after his four a.m. breakfast, with a single gunshot to the head. Roughly on the spot where tourists now pay $50 to have themselves photographed with wax dummies of Kim Kardashian at Madame Tussauds, Hubert's Museum once stood, a basement-level flea-circus dump on West Forty-Second Street that featured far more compelling tableaux, including a seedy "re-creation" of the Fifth Avenue brownstone where two hoarder siblings, the Collyer brothers, were found dead in 1947, surrounded by 120 tons of accumulated junk. And just south of there in the Garment District—source at the time of 95 percent of all clothing manufactured in the United States—porters piloting clothes racks jammed the sidewalks so densely that pedestrians were forced into the gutter. Thousands upon thousands of small-scale businesses occupied storefronts and anonymous office buildings where everything required to design and create and adorn apparel could be sourced, no specialty too exotic. There were dealers in pelts and feathers and rhinestones and ribbons and beads and embroidery and lace, and also shops selling little else besides hook-and-eye fasteners, zippers, or merrowing machines that the fashion designer Stephen Burrows used to frill the hems and seams of his dresses to resemble leaves of lettuce.

Down on the Lower West Side were the piers of the old Cunard lines, now derelict and largely vacant spaces, skeletal and poetic remnants of ocean travel's heyday, an era when the

Hudson churned with tugs and barges and maritime trade was booming, a time before the master builder Robert Moses erected the highways that would eventually sever the city from the lifeblood of its port and rivers. Far from abandoned, those hulks had been repopulated by men who cruised day and night in the shadows, wandering through reception halls and purser's offices and along stairs stripped of banisters, hopping over rotted floorboards—missing altogether in places to reveal the oily river below—passing like phantoms through beams of the ecclesiastical light drifting through open rooftops. With their jeans unbuttoned, asses and cocks exposed, often entirely naked, they fucked each other against walls or clustered in groups, cash and ID tucked into athletic socks for safety, and their presence in those places lent to a city characterized at the time as a desperate and provisional wreck an immemorial sense of human theater, and the dignified grandeur specific to ruins.

This is not to suggest that the decrepit city was in every case so romantic. It was filthy, also, and corrupt and largely lawless. To reach one good friend's apartment off Avenue C, I had to bypass boarded-up tenements where junkies with sledgehammers had punched through exterior walls to set up shooting galleries in the basement. Come evening, that friend latched her front door with paired deadbolts and a jimmy bar, and then secured the wooden shutters on her bedroom window with crosspieces cut from two-inch-by-four-inch planks. Once, when visiting another friend at his loft on the Bowery, I was chased up the stairs by a knife-wielding mugger, managing to outrun him only by taking three steps at a time.

o o o

IT WAS A MILD JUNE AFTERNOON in 1973 at roughly the time when, as I figured it, my old high school classmates must have been striding onstage at college commencement in mortarboards and gowns, collecting diplomas. I, by contrast, was herding a ragtag film crew onto Welfare Island, later known as Roosevelt Island, to shoot a self-scripted episode of a video series based on one of the Nancy Drew mysteries.

Portraying Carolyn Keene's sleuth heroine was a histrionic drag queen with a plush beard, caterpillar eyebrows, and a Method acting approach to the role. The videographer was a kink sex buddy of the pretty boy cast as Nancy's butch female friend George. The backdrop for this mostly inexplicable theatrical effort was the abandoned hulk of a smallpox hospital, a Gothic Revival spook house looming over the East River, both foreboding and somehow comical with, behind it on the near shore in Queens, a huge neon sign advertising Pepsi-Cola.

At some later point, it will interest me to learn about the thousands affected by the outbreak of the variola virus, how they were isolated and treated here in the nineteenth century, how that period ended when the hospital was shuttered almost exactly a century before this day in June. Three out of every ten of those infected died, a mortality rate that later reverberates when I come to know too much about plagues, and survivors were usually disfigured by scars and often left blind. Originally this island was named by and known to the Lenape people, whose fishing camps were on these shores, as Minnehanonck, a name essentially translatable as "nice to be here."

Paula Hyman at dawn on the Fifty-Ninth Street Bridge
Photo by Milton Sarris

A successful rebranding of the island using the name of Franklin D. Roosevelt will eventually be linked to a scheme to develop affordable housing there; before that it will first have been rechristened Blackwell's and later Welfare Island, although to us the name of the place was less relevant than its semi-abandoned state, which left it wide open for us to use as a film set without need of permits. The dilemma we faced that day was how to get across the river, since an aerial tram linking Manhattan to Roosevelt Island was still in the future. Until the bicentennial, when the tram scheme would be implemented, there was just one way to reach Welfare Island, and that was by climbing a steep stairway at First Avenue and crossing the Fifty-Ninth Street Bridge on a narrow steel-grille footpath. Moving single file, our group fell into line, up the stairs and over, first the cameraman with me behind him toting foil light reflectors, afterward someone hauling hatboxes and zippered garment bags, and finally a bunch of painted and dragged-up actors in outlandish getups, a group that to commuters speeding past must have looked as hapless as the doomful daisy chain in Bergman's *The Seventh Seal.*

Reaching our destination, some distance on foot from the bridge, we picked our way through rubble and set up, myself and a bunch of unruly amateurs cast in a video play adapted from a mystery written for adolescent girls. The script was no initiation into literature. An experimental extension of some two-act dramas I'd thrown together under the questionable influence of countless afternoon movie viewings and such Off-Off-Broadway productions by Jackie Curtis or Tom Eyen as I could afford to see, it was too sincere in approach to be proper pastiche, yet not altogether without an essential sense of its own absurdity. For now, what we all shared—the tech geek with the novel, state-of-the-art video portapak, volunteering his efforts and equipment; the actors stealing time from day jobs to emote; the makeup guy who had already started earning good money styling fashion shoots for the glossies—was a belief in what Truman Capote called the myth of the city.

In Capote's version of the city is the fairy tale, all strange rooms and strangers' illuminated windows; "steam-spitting streets"; an "idol-head with traffic-light eyes winking a tender green, a cynical red"; an enveloping realm into which one escaped the dull "greater reality of elsewhere" to find a place in which "to hide, to lose or discover oneself." I felt unaccountably purposeful and happy that day, and even with no road map for myself or any sense of what might become of this wacko videoplay, I knew that I was its author. In that sense, my compass was set.

Meanwhile the actor playing the teen girl detective had vanished. Shelly, the makeup guy—a chirpy Southern creature in overalls, fuck-me pumps, and pigtails—cheerily claimed to have spotted Nancy wandering among the discarded hospital bedsteads scattered in a truck bay at the back of the building. The hunky video guy claimed he had seen her heading for the reeds near the shore. The wardrobe director—a grumpy ex-monk from Maine who'd left his order and now specialized in unearthing dead clothing stock from forgotten shops—insisted Nancy had gone AWOL into the woods.

"If she fucks up the look, I'll kill her," said the ex-monk of Nancy's smart thirties touring outfit, a forest-green velvet skirt worn under a tweed hacking jacket and topped with a felt Robin Hood cap.

Just then Nancy strolled nonchalantly out from behind a shrub where the actor portraying her had hiked his skirt to take a leak. Back from the underbrush, he tidied his beard with a pocket comb and slipped into character as the nosy girl sleuth. Off camera, someone crumpled sheets of cellophane to produce the sound of a house fire that was central to the plot. Just as in the novel, we shot scenes of a mystery man darting from the conflagration, of Nancy poking around the crumbling building and happening upon the so-called Swedish diary. In the weeks to come we would film sequels to this effort, first *The Secret of the Old Clock,* then *The Message in the Hollow Oak,* and *The Mystery at Lilac Inn,* and screen them at free loft parties.

Nothing whatever came of this. None of us would earn a cent from the series, which was eventually erased when the video guy sold the valuable tape stock for reuse. Yet when I think about these people and this period, it is with a rush of affection for that time and place and the sense of having collaborated briefly in the creation of some inadvertent magic. Despite flubbed lines, fits of temper, lost mascara wands, and diva tantrums, for a moment those of us on the set formed a merry collective. It would disperse as fast as it had formed. In the following decade, after *The New York Times* reported early outbreaks of a mysterious new malady termed "GRID," or "Gay-Related Immune Deficiency," the scattered cast and crew of *The Clue in the Diary* would informally reconvene to join forces with the army of outcasts that, faced with a disease that crept up on everyone, mustered for its own survival. Knowing this I cannot see those early days as squandered. It was in that moment of innocence and camaraderie that we mirrored for one another values that would, as it turned out, sustain those of us who survived and yet were permanently marked by our confrontation with the facts of dying and death.

Still, far from considering myself a writer, at this point I was still pulling in rent money modeling for the fashion illustrator, conditioned to stand stock-still and hold a pose. It was a job whose passivity I found increasingly hard to tolerate in part because I was supporting myself by doing, essentially, nothing. Since drawing came easily to me, I briefly toyed with commercial illustration, though I saw that my heart wasn't in it when, after putting together a portfolio and showing it to an artists' agent, he pitched me on illustrating a children's book he'd been shopping to publishers. The book was to be set in a diner where customers and staff alike are anthropomorphized cats. I didn't much mind drawing those idiotic images, but when the agent sold the book to a publisher with my work passed off as that of his girlfriend, I took it as an omen.

Leaving home for good, I had requested just one thing from my mother: her IBM Selectric typewriter. It was not until much later that I understood the O. Henry nature of her sacrifice, when I discovered in the trunk saved from the fire some sodden pages from a typewritten journal she'd kept secretly and stowed away. The onionskin pages were still legible, but I never considered reading them, both because the pages rekindled the ache of her loss and because knowing her private thoughts when I had barely had time to know her felt intolerable.

The typewriter was a groovy seventies color, closer to avocado than jade, a desktop tank with a vertically rolling platen, margin stop buttons, and a patented "type ball" that eliminated the repetitive necessity, though also the visceral pleasure, of hitting the carriage return arm. While high school may not have done much for me in the way of overall development, it did leave me with at least one indispensable skill: touch-typing. Though I would never become an expert like my mom, I was faster than the hunt-and-peck types I'd encounter throughout my career, people career-tracked from infancy yet lacking this key skill and also, often enough, much interest in the material one produced on an IBM Selectric. That is, writing.

If I was not yet a writer, I was an insatiable lifelong reader, and in this New York provided me with a bonanza. Not only were street vendors of used books a fixture of most neighborhoods, but there was a six-block stretch of Fourth Avenue south of Fourteenth Street known as Book Row, and on it no fewer than three dozen establishments crammed to the rafters, and often bursting at the seams, with volumes on every conceivable and many an unimaginable subject.

Several of these places were daunting antiquarian enterprises, shelves stocked with volumes bound in gilded Morocco leather. Some were the bibliophile equivalent of Bogie's rag house, with wares overspilling from cardboard boxes, slumping out the doors, shoehorned onto rolling library carts chained at curbside and trundled inside each evening. Regardless, books, like much all else at the time, cost peanuts.

Guided by nothing but curiosity and chance, I spent my ready cash amassing books by the armload, prowling the dusty shelves at the Strand and Pelican, Louis Schucman and the Atlantic Book Shop and Ortelius and, away in another part of town, the fancier and more daunting Argosy. Early in the process, I unearthed a copy of a Gay Talese book that would serve as an occupational road map, since it was in *New York: A Serendipiter's Journey*—a collection of columns from Talese's earliest days at *The New York Times*—that the writer was found prowling the boroughs in search of stories fueled by an affinity, one I shared, for kooks and oddballs, marginal characters and curious folkways, for holdouts from a New York that was already largely vestigial.

I don't know who reads this book anymore; maybe no one. Even in the days I am talking about—when Talese was an ascendant star of the New Journalism, a bestselling author, a tabloid fixture, and a regular at literary bolt-holes like Elaine's—the book was semi-obscure. Yet its easy prose was oxygen and, as the book's author threaded the maze of the city, his reverence for the marginal felt as familiar as when I rescued some forlorn treasure at a thrift shop, its worth increasing in proportion to my ability to spot it.

I felt the same about so many literary gems scattered along Fourth Avenue, in carts and on shelves and sometimes on bargain tables outside the Strand, with its unprovable claim of having "18 Miles of Books." I prowled the tables of damaged on-sale books at temples to reading like Brentano's, the same establishment where Don Ameche met Gene Tierney in *Heaven Can Wait*. I found the occasional treasure to shoplift from a book nook on the seventh floor at Macy's, it being hardly worth mentioning that full-price books were beyond my financial grasp. It did not occur to me to patronize the unaffordable literary bookshops any more than it did to take cabs or eat at restaurants, and I irrationally avoided the public library system because a book became real to me only when I possessed it.

Chance thus led me to Gore Vidal's essays racked alongside a tattered copy of a volume by Sainte-Beuve, one of Vidal's heroes and which I also bought, though mostly for the handsome binding. I found a first edition of Christopher Isherwood's *The Berlin Stories* wedged alongside something deathless by Gide, probably *The Caves of the Vatican* (the movie rights to which, I read, had been bought by Andy Warhol). One jackpot afternoon when my modeling gig had wound down, I headed to Broadway and immediately, on a one-dollar book cart, came across a hardbound edition of Henry James's *The Princess Casamassima* that I struggled with afterward like a cartoon illiterate caught reading books upside down. Cash in pocket, I assembled a haul that day that included *Ozma of Oz*, the third volume in L. Frank Baum's celebrated series and the one in which Dorothy Gale realizes, as eventually we all do, that the prospects are livelier, after all, in the Emerald City than at home in Kansas with Uncle Henry and Auntie Em. I found a dog-eared paperback of Edmund Wilson's *Memoirs of Hecate County;* immaculate cloth-bound editions of Fabre's *Insects,* volumes one through three; and a jointly autographed copy of *The Indian Tipi,* written and illustrated by Reginald and Gladys Laubin, married anthropologists who traveled in the 1930s to the remote Dakotas and were adopted by the Lakota Sioux, and renamed One Bull and Good Feather Woman.

Reviewing this recollected list now, I think mostly of what, in my ignorance, I missed. There was Flannery O'Connor, yes, and Willa Cather and Sarah Orne Jewett and Henry Beston, yet none of the Russians. There were Jane and Paul Bowles because people I knew were reading them then, interchangeably (although only one produced work that would prove to be of enduring value). There were the Goncourt brothers mined for delectably obscure nineteenth-century Parisian gossip, but no Flaubert, and certainly not Proust until many years later. I read then as though quilting an education. I portaged books home in a canvas ice bag laden with volumes sometimes grabbed for no better reason than that they were dirt cheap, and that there was something about the cover that I liked.

As with the I Ching or one of Sol LeWitt's conceptual artworks, subconscious patterns formed themselves. "Make ten thousand random not straight lines," LeWitt once wrote in his instructions for a piece, and without exactly intending to, I was doing just that, laying the groundwork for an avocation I did not yet recognize as such and, when I picked up a trove of John O'Hara short stories, I read them as a journeyman carpenter might examine a drawer by a master joiner, studying how transitions dovetail, the uses of dialogue as exposition, simultaneously absorbing O'Hara's lifelong fixation with tracing the fault lines of class. I fell easily into the collections of obscure authors like McCandlish Phillips, whose nonfiction would never attain the cult status of Joseph Mitchell's, possibly because Mitchell was the far better writer (and, as it turned out, fabulist). I scoured medical texts because the workings of the human body fascinated me, and ethnographic volumes to further comprehend how humans function in groups. I read the works of people like the death-obsessed English writer and painter Denton Welch, whose hothouse roman à clef, *A Voice Through a Cloud,* was one of many books recommended to me by the Anglo-American couturier Charles James.

Is it natural at that age to take every good thing for granted? In the small metropolitan circles that I kept bumbling into, there were so many compelling characters it hardly occurred to me to question my fortune. I had heard a great deal about James in stories retailed to me by Horst P. Horst, the German-born photographer, and Valentine Lawford (known to all as Nicholas, his middle name), a British diplomat whom he'd met in 1938 and remained with until Lawford's death in 1991. I'd become acquainted with these two men—much as I had with Anita Loos—after writing Horst a fan note. Clueless and anything but experienced, I could not offer them much in return. Yet they promptly invited me to see them, and often again thereafter, at their home in Oyster Bay Cove, where I did my best to follow along as these two accomplished men carried on conversations about personages and events that seemed to have come from a far-off universe.

Horst's house, a short drive from my parents' place, was a low white structure of cinder block covered in stucco, its rooms arranged with objects collected or received over the decades: Augsburg chalices, Picabia drawings, Louis XVI fauteuils, Jean-Michel Frank tables, a tapa cloth screen presented to Horst by Coco Chanel. Even I recognized that the stories the men told had been often rehearsed, yet I eagerly took in ancient gossip about exotic characters like the Russian painter Pavel Tchelitchew or the aristocratic German photographer George Hoyningen-Huene or the sewing-machine

heiress Daisy Fellowes or the murderous socialite Ann Woodward or the Anglo-American socialite Emerald Cunard, who
had developed an improbable passion for Nicholas when he
was thirty and she seventy-five. Somehow, along the way, I'd
gotten hold of Cecil Beaton's acidulous diaries, which helped
me to keep up a score card, at least, of the types featured in
Horst's and Nicholas's society tales.

At the time I had no idea what to make of the knowledge
that Woodward had "accidentally" shot her blue-blood husband coming out of the shower after "mistaking" him for a
prowler, that the art historian John Richardson kept a secret
sex dungeon in Philadelphia for his BDSM antics, that Christopher Isherwood was a spanking aficionado. But there was
a literary lesson to be learned about the nature of gossip, its
life span and uses, since decades later a lot of what I heard at
Horst's table would be recycled as lascivious prattle in *Vanity
Fair* stories or fictionalized in romans à clef by the likes of
Dominick Dunne.

And it was thrilling, certainly, to feel a connection to
worlds I had only read about and could not imagine entering.
What is more, Nicholas occasionally made introductions. It
was through him that I met Charles James, who, as he was
quick to inform me, may have been a great artist but equally
a nutjob, prickly and umbrageous, given to tantrums and to
incinerating friendships over a grudge. The jewelry designer
Elsa Peretti later called James a commonsensical genius, but
you could not prove that by his disheveled lodgings at the
Chelsea Hotel, where I first paid a visit in 1974.

Painted on a glass-paneled door on the sixth floor were

Valentine George Nicholas Lawford

the words "Sound of Shape Studio"; beyond it was a ramshackle three-room suite in which Charles lived and labored in a cyclonic mare's nest, surrounded by half-dressed mannequins, bolts of fabric, ziggurats of books and slumping stacks of paper, armchairs with springs that came at you like a rectal thermometer. Snuffling through it all was an incontinent beagle named Sputnik. No matter how regularly Charlie refreshed the air with clouds of Guerlain's Habit Rouge, he never succeeded in subduing the reek.

What I encountered that first day was a small, mild man in his sixties, dressed in what I would learn was his "at home" uniform: an oversize white Oxford Brooks Brothers shirt, the collar popped and waist tightly cinched with a wide leather belt, chunky Candie's platforms from a discount shoe store on Fourteenth Street, and Jockey briefs. Charles was always vain about his legs.

And he was entertaining. Avuncular and irascible, mercurial and generous, he talked nonstop in a fluty accent that amalgamated his Chicago background with that of England, where he had been raised. In free-associative monologues, he insulted other designers, railed against his hated father (who he often claimed had had him raped at boarding school to toughen him up), grumped about his estranged ex-wife, gossiped about the ornately dysfunctional lives of society clients who, almost inevitably, remained loyal until, exhausted by his temperamental antics, they fired him—in the unlikely event that he hadn't fired them first.

Speaking about James years later, the oil equipment heiress Christophe de Menil, an enlightened arts patron and devoted client of his, said, "He gave me a freedom I will always cherish." What he provided to me was reading lists, written in his looping cursive, sent in the mail or else scribbled out while I perched at the Chelsea on whatever uncluttered horizontal surface I could find. There was the Welch, of course, but also Marguerite Yourcenar's *Memoirs of Hadrian* and that inevitable station of the cross in any education on the "Decadents," Huysmans's to me barely penetrable "Against Nature."

Throughout the brief years I knew him, Charles was almost unfailingly charming and would remain so—until the occasion when I cajoled him into loaning me a quilted satin evening jacket that was already, by then, by far the most celebrated work from his archive. For obscure reasons, I had decided I wanted to photograph the jacket on my younger sister, Dana, a lovely teenager with blond hair that fell in long pre-Raphaelite waves.

Harder than persuading Charles to loan the thing was convincing my sister—the only kid in our family to have thrived in school and carved out some semblance of a conventional existence—to pose. She agreed grudgingly and rode the train to Penn Station, where I met her carrying the jacket, which we then walked across town to the West Side Highway in a dry cleaner's bag. I was delighted that Charles had agreed to release the jacket from his studio and somewhat surprised since, once earlier, he had loaned it to the artist Antonio Lopez, who wore it out dancing and brought it back torn. (Miraculously Charles's faithful studio assistant, Homer Layne, managed to stitch it up.)

It was a gorgeous object, created in 1937 for Mrs. Oliver Burr Jennings, the wife of a major Standard Oil stakeholder whose grand house, Burrwood, happened to be just a short drive from my family's house, just over on Snake Hill Road in Cold Spring Harbor. The jacket was in some sense an eiderdown bed quilt reshaped and with sleeves attached, yet engineered so the feather thickness was variably distributed and allowed the wearer to move with ease. While James is often called the first American couturier, he is probably better understood as a sculptor than a dressmaker; in any case, it is no exaggeration to cite the jacket as being "among his most important works," as the Victoria and Albert Museum (which now owns it) does, or to refer to it as a "cult object." More important, it was a kind of prototype for the millions of down puffer coats that would eventually follow and, although James had hoped to translate the design into other materials for a mass market, in this as in so many of his other commercial aspirations, he failed.

That day we took it to the piers and shot a group of images of a bored, if cooperative, Dana in a variety of stilted poses before I put her back on the Long Island Rail Road to ride home. Returning the jacket to the Chelsea, I mentioned in an offhand way to Charles where we'd been, and his volcanic reaction showed to me a side of him far from that of the mild eccentric I thought I knew. After that, a frost settled over the relationship; the letters stopped coming and I never saw Charles again.

At about this same time, in the spring of 1975, Paula's superstylized Art Deco watercolors of women began to attract commercial attention. The tiny heads and attenuated limbs and raucously patterned dresses created using peel-off floral stickers from the five-and-dime were suited to the retro stuff department stores were hawking. Suddenly, the portfolio she'd been dragging around for a year began to generate advertising jobs and, soon afterward, appearances on the cover of the industry bible *Art Direction*.

The editor of that magazine was a person called Stanley Stellar. Given how casually people we knew shifted identity, I assumed Stanley Stellar's name was an invention. "He says it's real," said Paula, shrugging, after collecting her sketches one day from Elaine Richardson, Mr. Stellar's assistant.

Long before the drag-name game formula of first pet plus mother's maiden name became a mainstream parlor trick, my friends and I routinely amused ourselves with naming games. For me it was an easy way to procrastinate when I sat down at the Selectric, attempting to type my way into an avocation. Because I had not and would not for some time settle into what the *New Yorker* editor William Shawn later called my "natural way of writing," I filled pages with sentences that were mostly collections of pleasing, empty sounds. Without exactly thinking of this as "writing," I steeped myself in exotic juxtapositions, pairing the name of the doomed sorceress from Fellini's *Satyricon*—she who "could turn a stone into water or put out the stars"—with something commonplace, to arrive at "Oenothea Jones." I fetishistically listed names in notebooks, ready to be attached to stories I had yet to create, as though a name alone could call a character into being.

There were serious names and outlandish names and campy names and names that were mash-ups of credit rolls from old silent films, from vaudeville, from Golden Age Hollywood, from Off-Off-Broadway, and from the Ziegfeld Follies, where the stars had glorious monikers like Gladys

Glad or Nita Naldi or Billie Burke, names that blazed themselves onto marquees.

Around this time, I came up with a crackbrained idea for a play that used all the names I had lying around, a satire set in a show-business hotel populated by central-casting stereotypes from across the decades. There would be a moll, of course, a hardboiled detective, a nelly floor walker in the mold of Franklin Pangborn, a dastardly whiplash, a dragon lady, a battle-ax, a novelty twin-sister act. The names I devised for the latter two were so silly I could hardly resist them: Shamrock and Jamaica Kincaid.

When we first met, through Paula, at a small party she gave at her Murray Hill apartment, Elaine Richardson made a point of introducing herself with prim formality by her full name: Elaine Potter Richardson. It seemed to suit the skinny beanpole dressed in saddle shoes, a fifties poodle skirt, and a snug Breton striped fisherman's sweater. Disarmingly offhand for someone whom I would come to know as surgically observant, Elaine Potter Richardson had a breathy, girlish, disarmingly antic way of talking, as though constantly bemused or caught off guard. "Gosh!" was her all-purpose exclamation then and thereafter, her version of Andy Warhol's conversation-stopping "Great!"

It was far from obvious then that she had already begun scheming her way out of the backwater she found herself in as a reporter on the minor doings of the commercial art world. But it became clear soon enough that the Elaine Potter Richardson I met that evening, and would come to know well, had probably begun diagramming the literary landscape of New York the moment she arrived in this country from the Caribbean. Her ambition was masked by a persona that George W. S. Trow would later troublingly characterize, in a "Talk of the Town" story about the West Indian Day Parade, as "sassy," as though she were a real-life version of the stereotyped characters I was lampooning in my play.

We made friends quickly, Paula and Elaine and I, and for a time the three of us became inseparable. We hung out at her Murray Hill place or at ours in the Bronx, and together with Elaine I sometimes set out down Bedford Park Boulevard's long hill to the Southern Boulevard entrance of the New York Botanical Garden and from there to the hulking glass conservatory in the middle of the park.

This colossal neo-Renaissance heap of glass and steel was erected in 1902 in imitation of the nineteenth-century Palm House at the Royal Botanic Gardens in Kew. Though its lacy frame and acres of glass remained a structural wonder, by the early seventies the glass house was all but in ruins. Shattered, handblown windowpanes were crudely taped over with plastic. Jungle vines grown thick as forearms were muscling the iron crosspieces from their uprights. Specimens of bottle palms and Canary palms and Mexican palms and Chinese fan palms in the vast Palm Dome tilted and listed wildly, disorienting the rare souls who ventured into the forgotten jungle, where the sense of being lost in a rainforest was amplified by vapor plumes leaking from the irrigation pipes and dissipated in rainbow mists. Plans were underway at the time to raze the conservatory; if the necessary millions weren't found, the dome and flanking greenhouse wings were doomed. Yet for

Elaine and me the place was enchanted—evocative, she said, not of her country, arid Antigua, but rather of her mother Annie's birthplace, the lush and spooky island of Dominica, a volcanic rock north of the Grenadines. Dominica was also Jean Rhys's birthplace, a haunted, isolated place with no natural harbor, cold streams coursing through subterranean caverns, and where, in later years, dubious universities would crank out assembly-line medical degrees and which South American cartels would use as a transfer point for cocaine. For me the conservatory felt oddly familiar, reminiscent of the tumbledown Gold Coast structures of my teenage years, monuments that despite the money and effort spent to construct them were hardly less ephemeral, after all, than the air castles my father built.

Though the Murray Hill neighborhood where Elaine lived was still a transitional, nowhere area of the city—less cool even than the provincial Bronx—it did have an abundance of cheap restaurants. Hardly anyone yet called the area Curry Hill; fewer still among our friends earned enough to eat anywhere but in dives and Cuban Chinese diners. Elaine, though, had a full-time job with salary and benefits; Paula and I had some cash from our freelance gigs. So we arranged to meet one day for lunch at Philippine Garden, a place Elaine knew and where, she explained at the Botanical Garden, you could get a full meal for about five dollars.

Elaine had something important she wanted to discuss over plates of peppery chicken adobo with sides of rice and carrot salad and slices of what tasted like Wonder bread. It was her name. She found it prosaic and boring. She wanted something that might stand out as distinctive in a byline, a pseudonym for the articles she planned to write for magazines besides *Art Direction*, and for the books she would publish, and for a meticulously crafted alternative identity. Since I had plenty of names in my notebooks, I offered suggestions. Most were from the lists I kept. Each in turn was dismissed by Elaine. Why I felt so determined about this I don't know, but I kept going until finally, as a joke, I offered a name from my little satirical playlet: "What about Jamaica Kincaid?"

"That," she said, fixing me with a withering look, "is too, too stupid."

It was true. What serious person would choose to be known by the name of a character from an imaginary vaudeville sister act in an unproduced play by a writer so obscure he doesn't yet know he is one? The name Jamaica Kincaid, we agreed as we split the bill and prepared to leave, was colonialist, stupidly exotic, too campy, had none of the gravitas she apparently had in mind. And that—as far as the two of us would ever discuss—was the end of that.

The next week, when Paula went up to the *Art Direction* offices to drop off some new portfolio drawings for Elaine, she was startled to learn there was no such person on the premises.

"Are you sure?" she asked.

"Yes," the receptionist said. "Or . . . do you mean Jamaica Kincaid?"

o   o   o

AROUND THIS TIME, in the way things seemed to occur, would always occur—as I now see it—I will bumble into another kind of unexpected employment, in this instance in a new place—one that, although I cannot possibly have known it, would soon and for a surprisingly long time thereafter shape the contours of city nightlife and, ultimately, of the world beyond it.

Paula heard about the job from her friend and my acquaintance Andrea Lucidity, earlier our tipster to the wonders of Bogie's. Andrea knew of a new club—a new kind of club, she said—where there might be jobs for both of us. What the jobs entailed exactly was unclear and did not become less blurry when we arrived for our interviews at a tenth-floor loft in a midblock building on West Twenty-Fifth Street. At one time a sewing-machine factory, the loft was modest in size, perhaps 1,500 square feet, a bare T-shaped space with a long rectangle as its upright and a short, broad intersecting bar containing two small cubicles: a supply room and an office.

Andrea mentioned that the loft was being renovated as some sort of private dance place and, when we arrived for our interview, contractors with nail guns were still installing gray contract carpeting on a series of banked plywood risers by the south-facing window wall. It would be a while before high tech was formalized as a style, but its stripped-down elements were already being deployed at the club-to-be, with low banquettes and a raised deejay booth and, between them, a dance floor framed by structural cast-iron columns.

The place was to be called the Tenth Floor, for self-evident reasons, and would later attain semi-mythical status, largely thanks to *Dancer from the Dance,* Andrew Holleran's fevered novel about gay male life in its last great flowering before AIDS. In the book the club was called the Twelfth Floor, but otherwise rendered more or less accurately as a sacred new kind of space, run by two bearded guys, each named David, each dressed in the 501 jeans, flannel shirts, and work boots that were the gay uniform of that moment. The club's owners belonged to a type I hadn't previously encountered, slick and confident professional gay men who clearly had money. Pines queens, they were called, after the prosperous gay summer colony on Fire Island, and they were a sharp contrast to the penniless bohemians we'd been running around with—not least because many had begun taking up bodybuilding, still a relatively new phenomenon at the time.

When Holleran eventually wrote about the Tenth Floor he characterized it as a church for the "strange democracy" of dance, and—absent the democratic part—I can see that. In a sense the dance floor resembled a nave and the raised deejay booth a pulpit from which, Friday to Sunday of each week, a blue-eyed black man named Ray Yeates assumed the mantle of a mystic. Seldom leaving the booth for a break, Ray spun disco and proto-house music for six hours at a stretch, pissing in a bottle and often, occasionally so stoned on Quaaludes that he nodded out at the turntable.

Whatever there was about the Tenth Floor that could be romanticized as churchy was far from apparent in its unfinished industrial state; what we saw at our interview was an unpromising dump. And the interview itself amounted to little more than us stifling laughter when the Davids asked about our availability, and then concealing our shock when they mentioned that the salary was $40 a night. At this point our rent for the Bronx apartment had risen to $78 a month,

Guy Trebay

which we split. The pay was in cash. Could we start on opening night in two weeks?

Who are these people, we asked each other when we hit the street, so stunned by the offer we barely dodged the clothes racks hurtling our way. What is this place? And more important, why hire us to work at some club catering to a crowd that, as we soon learned, was overwhelmingly white and male and uniformly attractive and drawn from a caste of successful professionals we had never encountered: closeted guys with "straight" jobs at banks or white-shoe law firms who either shed their daytime suits for the club uniform—flannel shirts, tight tees, laced construction-worker boots, bomber jackets over hoodies—or else were representatives of a novel cadre of creative directors, photographers, agents working in jobs where it was possible to be both successful and openly gay. Some, a very few, as Holleran wrote, were "film stars and rock stars, and photographers . . . people like Calvin Klein or Andy Warhol," and some were "rich Parisians," although how Holleran knew that is a mystery. They were people "who might not even know each other, but knew who each other were," he wrote, and it was true that in a certain cultish way you could consider the wild-child *Vogue* model Apollonia van Ravenstein or the wraithlike celebrity hairdresser Ara Gallant, dressed always in leather and a studded Muir cap, celebrities. Grace Jones, who once came to the Tenth Floor with her brother and took to the dance floor almost naked, was, although not yet, certain to become universally famous.

We, on the other hand, were patently nobodies, and it

seems obvious now that was largely why we'd been hired. Young and ornamental, we so little resembled the usual Tenth Floor clientele that we were easy to distinguish as the help. Paula by then had taken to wearing her hair cropped short and dyed a stark henna red, eyebrows shaved off in imitation of the affectless new Warhol star Jane Forth. Her everyday wardrobe alternated between thrift-shop frocks and carpenter jeans worn with men's shirts knotted at the waist and wood-soled platforms from Goody Two Shoes. I had by now lopped off my long hair and gotten a cheap barber to give me a Marine buzz cut, which I peroxided over the kitchen sink, double processing it to achieve a radioactive shade of platinum blond. My uniform consisted of olive-drab fatigues bought cheaply at Hudson's Army-Navy store, work boots, and a thrifted "Meet the Beatles" T-shirt from the band's first American tour.

Paula and I alternated between the coat check and a juice bar, where it was our job to top off the big aluminum bowl with a fruit-and-nut mixture poured from industrial-size sacks. Since the club had no liquor license, we also dispensed free sugary juices. The work was by no means taxing and, after the club had been open awhile and we were familiar with the owners, the clientele, and the routine, I did less and less of it. Using the pretext of circulating to empty ashtrays (people still smoked freely in all public settings), I snuck onto the dance floor whenever I could. And if the experience was for me not religious or sacral, it felt transformative; each time, I joined a rush of sweaty limbs and torsos, merging with them. Time collapsed on the dance floor, so that in that ecstatic place you were in the present and simultaneously the past, at the

Tenth Floor but also in the alley outside Golden Crest Records with L'Wraine, and also in the living room of our apartment when I was a young child, folded into my young parents' bodies as they swayed to Harry Belafonte's calypso tunes.

When Paula and I first met, we sometimes went dancing at Tamburlaine, a Chinese-restaurant-turned-Latin-club with a big plastic palm tree in the middle of the dance floor, joining a motley assortment of art-school kids in thrift-store clothing who all crowded the dance floor at precisely six p.m. and danced nonstop for three hours in accordance with the club's policy of opening its doors to a young crowd hoping to attract a lively clientele to what was a nightlife dead zone on the East Side. We danced nonstop until nine p.m.; after that, you had to buy a drink that none of us could afford.

And Paula and I danced all the time in the apartment, together or with friends, taking turns resetting the player arm on our portable stereo, returning the needle again and again to the opening notes of "Girl You Need a Change of Mind," moving across the old parquet floor like the kids we saw on *Soul Train,* caught up in the thrill of a shivering cymbal, the run of stuttering piano bass notes, the trombone wailing, and then the soaring vocal line of Eddie Kendricks's unearthly falsetto singing "Oo-la-la-la-la-la-la. Girl you need a change of mind."

o o o

WHY DANCE HAS THIS transporting effect I will never know, yet I don't question it or its power any more than I do my affinity for spaces where people gather to do it, or my sense of them as somehow consecrated. They are, as I imagine it, like the clearings where shamans guide believers to a welcome oblivion, not to take you from this world, but to keep you in it rapturously. Or so it seems inside the Tenth Floor, where an intense and possibly unprecedented sort of tribal bonding occurs every night. Initially, as a worker, I am not part of these rites any more than I am a member of this tribe. That's not the worst thing. In fact, it is to some degree providential, since so many of the clubgoers I watch every night—the men I pour oversweet juice for and serve salted nuts to—will never see forty, while I as the perennial observer, present and yet invisible, lost in the watching, will survive.

And this feeling will recur again and again in all sorts of unlikely places. I think of a grimy Harlem club, say, where the venerable hoofers Honi Coles and Chuck Green lay out a scrap of Masonite onstage and sprinkle it with sand before performing wizardly soft-shoe for a tightly gathered group of admirers. I think of an improvised catwalk formed when rival posses flank a "runway" in a catering hall in Queens rented by the mother of the House of Ultra Omni so the "children" of various competing ballroom houses can spin and dip and duckwalk and throw down from midnight until daybreak to remixed versions of "The Ha Dance." I think of a beaten-earth arena I visit once on a Crow Indian reservation in the Rocky Mountain Front Range, where grass dancers in full regalia crouch and spin and whirl to the twined wails of Lakota drummers, their keening warriors' voices causing what science calls piloerection, hair standing up on your head.

It goes without saying that all of this is as radically unlike the dance forms that will eventually dominate life in a digital age, the thousands of three-minute routines performed for a camera and one million of your closest social-media friends, as random dick pics are from Herman's ornately staged photo-booth tableaux vivants. Dance—or anyway, communal dance—is a haven for me and, as the weeks go on at the Tenth Floor, I start sneaking away from the juice bar more often, neglecting the filthy ashtrays to pause alongside a column, scoping out the dance floor until eventually and tentatively slipping onto it.

This is made irresistibly easy by Ray Yeates, who will sometimes begin what Andrew Holleran terms a "string of songs" with the slow groove of "Giving Up" by Zulema and then cut to a Top 40 Spinners tune, veering to the club hit of the season, a First Choice tune that blares into being with a siren and a "calling all cars" alert, a warning that some fugitive lover man on the loose is "armed and extremely dangerous." Hokey as the song may be, it magnetizes everyone to the dance floor. Putting down whatever it is I'm doing, I sneak onto it, too.

If I am anything but inconspicuous, with my bleached hair and punk getup, I convince myself that no one is looking. It is a good trick, this ability to render myself invisible, and eventually, as it happens, I will turn it into a tool of the trade I fall into, as useful a quality for a writer to have as the habitual watchfulness I also possess and an ease at investing myself occupationally in the feelings of others while, in my own life, I stand stubbornly apart from the narrative.

Except for Paula, the deejay, and some of the club's more celebrated patrons, I know hardly anyone here by name and am so apparently unrepresentative of the type the place attracts that I feel like an anomaly, an outsider who happens to find himself inside. In many ways this will always be true of me.

If there is one notable individual at the Tenth Floor, it is a shaven-headed man with a taut muscular body and a kinetic dragonfly intensity. Whereas most dancers pair up, form clusters, sweat-soaked and theatrical, their T-shirts stripped off and tucked in the back pockets of 501 jeans, hands cupping popper bottles, this man keeps to himself. Or, rather, he skitters across and around the dance floor, guided by the music but apparently also by beats seemingly only he can hear. He flits through the crowd; moving to its perimeter; at times seeming to hover above the dance floor, so rapid are his high-stepping and leg-pumping movements. Occasionally, head thrown back, he pistons in place until, guided by some unknown signal, he suddenly releases himself as if to break free of gravity altogether, caroming off columns and walls. "Music ran our legs and we danced," the poet Nathaniel Mackey wrote somewhere. To my mind, he could have been describing this man: "Gone up into air, aura, atmosphere."

Obviously, the guy is stoned, though I don't fully recognize this as I study him—his name, I eventually learn, is Darnell Young, and he is an artist, professional dancer, and occasional performer in porn films—and shyly pick up some of his dance moves. Without him being in any way aware of this, I memorize what he does, to be practiced at home and adapted to the limitations of a gangly physique so much different from his.

Because our pay at the Tenth Floor more than covers the monthly nut, and because the place is open only Fridays to Sundays, Paula finds herself free to paint all week. I can scribble away at videoplays with which I still have no idea what to do. Both of us are left with ample time to go trashing, which, like thrifting, has been elevated by our pals into something of an art form. One or two of them even go on to establish serious careers as antiquarians, though we all know that what they resell as "vintage" is junk found at curbside.

We also share their general knowledge of bulk collection days and Department of Sanitation routes for every neighborhood and borough—information not readily obtained in the days before the internet—as well as more specific data about the choicest streets to work, intel we husband as though it were the map to Bluebeard's treasure. Certain of us favor the side streets on and around Central Park West, where a population of cultured European refugees—many driven here during the Second World War—has started to dwindle, leaving behind sprawling places jam-packed with midcentury treasures not yet marketed as such. Whether out of aesthetic ignorance or obliviousness, the inheritors of these prewar behemoths in citadels like the Dakota, the Century, the El Dorado, the Langham, the Beresford, the Majestic, or Rossleigh Court tend to toss not just prizes like the occasional Mies van der Rohe daybed or Donald Deskey desk lamp but also large quantities of middling Art Deco stuff that has lately begun to find a market among decorators.

Typical of me, the business side of this holds little interest. If the hunt is exciting, the more so is the random exploration of a city that—while I was substantially raised here and feel for it a New Yorker's reflexive chauvinism—I have yet to vascularize with experiences that make it part of my adult being. This will happen, gradually and eventually, as I come to spend much of my professional life losing and finding myself again

Darnell Young, 1972

in the byways and on the verges, in Manhattan's underground realms and also in the terra incognita of the boroughs. That has hardly begun at this point, when most city neighborhoods are still terrain to be personally explored and mapped, later to be treasured for qualities seldom noted on maps or inventories of civic wonders. Mostly these are places that, like the city itself, are slumping toward desuetude.

New York, in short, is on the skids, and if its inhabitants are abandoning it in droves, who can blame them? Even in the fanciest sections sidewalks glisten with ominous carpets of shattered glass, residue of smash-in car thefts. The inevitable hand-scrawled "No Radio" signs posted inside windshields seem as plaintive as pointless. Manhattan in particular is hit hard during the early seventies, when determined burglars undeterred by a battery of security measures—deadbolts, door jammers, crossbars, kickbars, jimmy-proof metal flanges wedged into door frames—have made locksmithing a land-office business. Not that their efforts make any difference. When the fortress entryway to one friend's fifth-floor walk-up in the East Village proves impregnable, the crooks bypass it altogether; using a chisel, they gouge a hole through the plaster, reach through the wall, and unlatch the door.

Far from having our stuff walk away, we experience a surreal reverse of fortune. One night leaving for the club, we bid goodbye to our new roommate, a stealth slut and interior design student we refer to, behind his back, as Ugly Stanley. When we leave to catch the D train downtown that winter evening, Ugly Stanley is waiting for his boyfriend to get there, flipping through the latest copies of *Honcho* and *Drummer* propped up in a makeshift platform bed hammered together from plywood and two-by-fours. Gone by nine p.m., we won't return until well after the final stoned club stragglers are shoveled onto the crotchety freight elevator at the Tenth Floor; until Paula has returned the last identical leather bomber to its owner; until I've rebagged the leftover snack mix—a health code violation if ever there was one—and scoured the serving bowls of their nut dust coating.

That is to say it is three a.m. when we finally get paid out. David 1 or is it David 2 peels off four tens from a thick wad, hands them over, and says goodnight. Then, in the zombie state of all nocturnal workers, we ride the elevator to the street and bend into the bitter wind that blows off the Hudson, making our wordless, bedraggled way to the subway. It's too cold to talk, and I don't know what Paula's thinking. My own thoughts are focused on stripping off my smoke-rank club clothes, taking a quick shower, and collapsing into bed.

The Bronx is even more dead than Manhattan at this hour, with only the occasional forlorn yellow light burning in the window of some tenements along the way from the subway to our place. It's a walk that would give anyone jitters, not because we fear crime—what mugger is dumb enough to be out at this hour?—but because in its desolation the slumbering city seems as though it may never revive.

"Hurry," I say impatiently to Paula, who is dragging.

"Go on if you want to walk ahead," she says. "My dogs can't go any faster after six hours in these heels."

Once home, we mount the stoop, happy for a change that

we live on the building's first floor. Paula leans against the wall, exhausted, while I fish out a key, which turns easily in the lock. As I push the door open, we are greeted by the stale though welcomingly familiar must of a radiator-heated apartment and then abruptly pitched into an episode of *The Twilight Zone.*

Can this be the right place? Largely empty when we left home, the apartment is now fully furnished. It is as though we have stumbled into Narnia. Here in the darkened living room I make out a dresser. A chifforobe and a glass-front china cabinet stand in a corner, near a wardrobe with a mirrored door in which I'm startled by my own reflection. The formerly naked windows are dressed with cretonne curtains and, tiptoeing from room to room, we find all similarly arranged. Peering into Ugly Stanley's room, I see an upholstered wing chair draped with a tangle of clothes beside a dowdy maple four-poster in which Ugly Stanley and his latest boyfriend, Tony, lie with their legs entwined.

It is too early to wake them, so Paula and I creep into beds, now tidily made, that eight hours ago were mattresses on the floor. And we crash. Ugly Stanley and his lover are gone by the time we awaken, and so most of the day passes before we learn that it is Tony we can thank for our unexpected windfall. It was Tony who, on the way to the supermarket, happened upon the entirety of an elderly neighbor's apartment as it was hauled to the street.

"Ella pasó," Tony explains. "She croaked."

The building's super had pitched what would seem to have been all the accumulated junk of this stranger's existence, the material evidence of a life, out on the street. From what we can deduce, whoever she was, the woman was a widow or at any rate unmarried, since there is nothing from the trove—the boxes of dresses and shoes; the aluminum Revere cookware pots; the assortment of sad Reader's Digest Book Club anthologies in gilt-tooled faux-leather bindings; the "Oriental" figurine lamps with fringed silk shades—to suggest a masculine presence.

It was all there, the remnants of decisions made, goods worried over in shops and weighed for value, stolid stuff perhaps purchased on an installment plan, all the autographical trash we cling to until the time comes when whatever small value our possessions hold for us disappears. Carted off on bulk collection day, this stranger's objects would have joined the slag heap of anonymous lives had Ugly Stanley not dispatched Tony to Food Mart to shoplift some chopped chuck for dinner. So for a time, until Ugly Stanley moves out and Paula and I amiably drift apart, we will live comfortably in these rooms filled with a dead stranger's things.

And for me—with the innately scavenging nature I've honed since leaving home to live on my own, with an ever-fiercer sense of seeking my way unaided, with the habit of learning to make do with what others find little use for—this melancholy jackpot, found and then, by us, abandoned again, serves as a counterpoint to James Baldwin's portentous observation that "nothing is fixed, forever and forever and forever."

Why expect things to be? Already at twenty-two, I've got a better-than-average acquaintance with loss, the beginnings of an understanding, which proves essential to me in the long run, that there had never been any real foundation for the promise my parents' lives seemed to hold. The boats and cars and houses was just stuff, destined to be reclaimed, sold, or incinerated. None of it had been mine to inherit in the first place. My true inheritance, when I think about it, was my own unwitting exile. Sent off with a jumbled, random assortment of traits in my genetic kit bag—most serviceably a wild curiosity and the flint of ambition—most of what I needed I probably already had. My skepticism, for instance—so deep as to amount to a character flaw—developed as a natural defense against the more outlandish of my father's fictions, and not just that of a great imaginary Polynesian adventure incubated in the Bronx.

Many of his embroideries I look upon now with affection and forgiveness, without forgetting that the greater percentage of what is passed off as fact in our lives falls apart under scrutiny. Dubiety may not be the same as truth-seeking. But it is a useful tool in its pursuit.

Random things, in any event, light up in memory; scattered recollections fuse and collide. I am seven and standing at the counter of a candy store a short walk from our apartment on Archer Road. In the pocket of my shorts is a quarter's allowance, enough to buy a package of Pixy Stix and two issues of *Adventure Comics*.

We are living in Parkchester and will until I am in second grade, when my father quits his day job as an ad salesman for *Parade* magazine and moves us first to a modest house on the North Shore of Long Island and then, when the money from Hawaiian Surf starts to roll in, to that place impressive enough to house a country club. It is a long way, yet little real distance at all, to that place from our first apartment: five rooms on the top floor of a solid seven-story structure, redbrick and adorned with terra-cotta sculptures, one of nearly thirteen thousand such apartments spread across 171 similar buildings ranging from seven to twelve stories and comprising a small and largely insulated city of its own. Developed on land that the Metropolitan Life Insurance company bought from the Catholic Church following the Great Depression, Parkchester was inspired first by the City Beautiful movement and, as I'll learn, by certain modernist precepts Le Corbusier forwarded about towers in a park.

As a boy I obviously cannot know it in this way. So for me instead it is a kingdom invisibly moated from the surrounding city, a private realm whose tidy grounds are maintained by an army of uniformed caretakers. Treed walkways and clipped lawns, which occupy fully two-thirds of all the available land, create a sense of security that must have felt close to miraculous for the original inhabitants of this development, working-class people recently emerged from the Great Depression, a calamity that shadowed lives for decades, no matter what anyone did to erase memories of soup kitchens, breadlines, and "home" children farmed out to strangers or orphanages until their parents could afford to reclaim them, the way my mother and her brother had been.

Most afternoons when school lets out, I meet my friend Billy in the lobby of his building and we wander, roaming the walkways linking all the buildings, exploring our insular universe though never venturing beyond a well-delineated perimeter where the real, the grittier, the more menacing Bronx begins. Peering northwest toward East Tremont Avenue and

White Plains Road we can just make out, past those lines of demarcation zones that seem intriguingly chaotic, dangerous, messy, a sooty wasteland cut through by railway tracks. The view is as visually jumbled as Parkchester is stable and serene. From my bedroom window facing west, I can look out over cracked concrete backyards, rows of run-down frame houses squeezed right up against the borders of the Parkchester complex, segregated from it on the Archer Road side by a sharp grade change and a palisade of cyclone fencing.

Sometimes, Billy and I peer through the diamond-patterned chain links at the disorder of another kind of existence: wet clothes flapping on slack lines, mongrels chained to poles that are anchored in concrete-weighted buckets, crammed onto fire escapes with bicycles, rubber plants, and washtubs jumbled on them yet never with any sign of humans. Who are these others living on that side of the fence? From what we overhear, they may be Italians who somehow overspread the boundaries of Little Italy on Arthur Avenue. Or they could be Puerto Rican families or even the black people who we, as children, do not know are prohibited from renting in Parkchester by racist covenants.

Billy and I blast through the complex, easing into the refrigerator cool of Macy's, ride the escalators to the basement and the fabric department, where, beneath the counters, stock drawers deep enough for scrawny seven-year-olds to squeeze into while playing hide-and-seek are. We dare each other sometimes to venture down a certain dimly lit service ramp that leads to a janitorial depot, a place we name the Land of a Thousand Halls. There, in a recessed doorway that smells

Metropolitan Oval, Parkchester, the Bronx, 2022

of stale urine, we enact blood-brother rituals, pretending to hypnotize each other, ceremonially eating dirt or leaves.

If our parents seem unconcerned about our absences this may not be so unreasonable given how many lifetimes ago this all took place and how, even many decades on, it will remain acceptable practice to send your young kids out into the city on their own. This will all change, of course, one spring morning in 1979 when Etan Patz is abducted on Prince Street in SoHo as he heads to meet the school bus for the very first time. With the vanished six-year-old goes something that remained, inexplicably, innocent about the city for much longer than you might have imagined possible.

Our wanderings never feel lonesome because everywhere we are chaperoned by the companionable, if inanimate, presence of hundreds of terra-cotta ornaments integral to the architecture of the complex—at cornices, over doorways, inset atop the arched passageways that cut street-to-street through buildings like Venetian sotoportegos.

The beautiful superfluity of these ornamental sculptures worked into the fabric of the place lends it all a kind of fairy-tale quality in a child's eyes—these bas-reliefs and roundels depicting a seemingly random assortment of workers at their tasks: There are firemen, fishermen, jesters, troubadours, muscular oilmen wielding a massive wrench. There are skiers slaloming vertically down the edges of buildings. Mermaids repose above lintels. Dutch girls in wooden shoes are tucked into roundels above doorways. On a small raised plaza giving onto a passageway is a polychrome tondo depicting two housewives of the thirties, a breeze lifting the hems of their housedresses, their heads tilted toward each other to gossip, so engrossed that one is about to drop her knitting along with the yapping dog in her lap.

There are dolphins, penguins, deer, ducks, antelope, toucans, fluttering doves set into plaques in the walls. Centering a lushly planted oval that anchors the radial street plan of the complex is a large pool of water adorned with a fountain in which a group of bronze mermen lounge on ventral or dorsal sides, lips spouting water in powerful jets. Although getting to the fountain involves crossing several streets and brings me out of what instinctively feels like a safe radius from home, I come anyway to Metropolitan Oval just to stare at the big bronze whale breaching at one end of the pool, more mermen riding pillion on its upturned tail.

Often I don't call on Billy at all and set out alone. And while I have no way of knowing this yet, this roaming substantially sets a pattern I'll maintain of wandering the streets on my own, and many foreign cities, miles and miles, clocked on foot, often as though somehow it were possible to walk right out of yourself.

From the candy store, I head directly to the post office, reached through a passageway linking Wood Road to the dead end of West Avenue. First I make my selection of lime Pixy Stix, ripping the straw with my teeth, emptying the contents into my mouth all at once for the sour-sweet burn of sugar powder on my tongue. And I linger over the latest installment of the Green Lantern racked with the other comic books I'm discouraged from reading, fake deliberating over whether also to splurge on a Bachman pretzel rod from a lidded jar, or else a piece of halvah, marbled, crumbly, and mystifyingly oily, when what I am in fact doing is surreptitiously eyeing the covers of the tabloids that are similarly unwelcome in our house. From the covers of both the *Daily News* and the *Daily Mirror* blare block-lettered headlines about the latest dastardly exploits of a home-grown terrorist who holds the city in his grip.

It has been years—in fact, the whole of my young life—since the Mad Bomber started his campaign of terror by planting bombs in or near Con Ed buildings, the second hidden in an old woolen sock. Footwear recurs as a Mad Bomber motif, frequently used to loop bombs over railings or knot them to pipes with attached notes addressed to the *New York Herald Tribune* imploring its readers to "Cry Out for Justice for Me."

There will be other nefarious deeds and further bombs (thirty-three in all) planted in offices, restrooms, Grand Central Terminal, and Radio City Music Hall during a holiday showing of *White Christmas* (starring Rosemary Clooney and Bing Crosby). As it happens, the Mad Bomber's methods are rudimentary and not lethal. When the Christmas bomb detonates—it is hidden in the upholstery of an orchestra seat, row 14—four people suffer injuries requiring treatment at a first aid station behind a lobby concession stand. Theatergoers near the incident are later provided with new seats from which to enjoy the remainder of the movie, followed by a Rockettes spectacle.

George Metesky—that is the Mad Bomber's name—is plainly a sad sack and, in my reading, most likely queer. A bachelor, he lives in Waterbury, Connecticut, with his two unmarried sisters. Were I a satirist writing his tale, I might think twice before assigning him the job he held at Con Edison as a "generator wiper." But there it is. There is nothing amusing, however, about the accidental boiler backfire that blasted George Metesky to the floor one morning, hot gases from the explosion burning and scarring his lungs. When he developed first pneumonia and then, eventually, tuberculosis, doctors found him unfit to work. His disability claim was initially denied on a technicality, and then several further times on appeal. Metesky, possibly not the most stable man to begin with, drew the paranoid conclusion that he had been gamed by a crooked system. In truth, he most likely was.

No one could condone George Metesky's actions, yet even as a kid, I sensed there was something more to the story of the Mad Bomber than it appeared. Now I understand the need for a lone bogeyman, someone to shoulder the blame for a broader anxiety gripping both city and country. As it happens, the Mad Bomber's spree is contemporaneous with *Godzilla,* a prime cinematic parable of Cold War nuclear terror, and anyone my age can recall elementary school classes interrupted for duck-and-cover bomb drills, remembers kneeling in hallways outside classrooms, hands clasped behind heads bent to the floor. What was the point of those exercises, some early version of active-shooter drills? Surely it was not to save us from death in the event of nuclear attack.

One evening my parents park me with our next-door neighbors while they go to a party at the Plaza Hotel, where my godmother's father is the general manager. Flipping on the TV to a showing of *The Crawling Eye,* the neighbors sit me on the sofa with their children and we all watch as two young sisters, Anne and Sarah Pilgrim—one plagued by the random telepathic gift that was so often a B-movie plot point—detect the existence in a small Swiss resort of killer extraterrestrials. The aliens live, if that is the word, atop the local mountain beneath what will turn out to be a radioactive cloud.

Despite being so stylized in its effects, the film could have come straight out of the early German expressionist canon; it's a conventionally clunky nuclear-age parable. The horror menacing the local canton, as the trailer proclaims, to "wreak death and destruction too horrible to behold," is somehow more disturbing than almost anything I can recall from the period. An enormous, pulsating eye disembodied and crawling on weird tentacles, it inhabits "its own silent world that no man can penetrate," as the movie trailer said. And for years afterward, as much as I am haunted by the image of that terrifying eye crawling through the snow, I am also troubled by the childish conviction that there are no born monsters, not really, though there are unquestionably those condemned to inhabit impenetrable silent worlds.

Metesky is, in his own way, haunted. Always prone to paranoid lapses, he reaches the conclusion that his superiors colluded with Con Ed to cheat him out of his insurance and then begins to spiral, retreating to a shed in the garden of his suburban dwelling, tooling components for his homemade bombs and, eventually, after detonating the first few devices, composing increasingly unhinged pleas to an unwitting public to "see" and "understand" him and to sympathize with what he identifies, in all capital letters, as his "CAUSE."

Written in unusual red ink, these seemingly glaring clues to the Mad Bomber's identity somehow elude the notice of the police and FBI investigators for fully sixteen years before an alert clerk at Con Edison spots one of Metesky's letters, redacted and published in *The New York Times,* and recalls having read a similar one buried in a workman's compensation file. She sensibly observed that not only did the claimant in the letter rail against unspecified "INJUSTICES" resulting from his "PERMANENT DISABILITY," but he did so in capital letters, using red ink.

Metesky is dressed in pajamas when the authorities turn up at the door of his Waterbury house one morning in 1957. Though he does not resist arrest, he asks for enough time to change into his good, double-breasted suit. Metesky is tried and convicted and committed for life to the Matteawan State Hospital for the Criminally Insane. A $25,000 reward long posted for his detection and capture is paid out. The reward goes not to the canny clerical worker who identified the "Mad Bomber," however; it is presented instead to a police detective on the case, a man who happens to live in a G line apartment on the third floor of our building on Archer Road.

The Parkchester post office is entered through oak double doors. Near them stands a desk where customers can stamp outgoing letters and open their mail. Hung above it is a bulletin board. Mounted on it is a ring-punched binder holding updates to the FBI's "Ten Most Wanted" list. While technically these so-called identification orders are tools of public awareness, of tipoff and detection, all that is to me incidental. It is not that I would mind aiding in the capture of some random terrorist, bank robber, or murderer, collecting a reward and basking in the ensuing celebrity. What draws me here to check in on the latest fiends and fugitives, however, to note their descriptions and memorize their scars and identifying marks, is a feeling of connection. To the usual overheated imagination of a seven-year-old, let us add this. I feel I somehow know these people. I sense that not much more separates me from them than fate.

And, as it happens, I will be back at a post office some fifteen years on, once more checking out the flyers. This time around I am looking for my sister's face. It feels important to say here that much of what follows about my sister Laura is not my story to tell. I can hardly avoid it, though, because omitting it will leave too conspicuous a hole in this narrative. The facts are there. In the summer when Laura is twenty-one and I am twenty-two, she commits armed robbery and is arrested and sent to jail. I post bail. The bond is $10,000 in cash. This amounts to every cent I have saved from the time I was given my first bankbook.

The crime is sufficiently crackbrained that you might think it was a stunt. But it is not a gag. With her boyfriend waiting curbside in a sedan that will prove ridiculously easy to identify by its out-of-state license plates, Laura enters the pediatric office a paternal uncle by marriage maintains inside his house in Babylon. It is sometime in the early afternoon. Office hours have ended. It is the hour when my uncle customarily reviews patient records in an anteroom to a solarium that serves as his examining room. I do not know for a fact but can easily imagine him looking up in surprise, although not necessarily in alarm, when Laura unexpectedly walks in. That is, until she pulls out a handgun.

There is a small powder room just inside the second of two

doors in the foyer reserved for the use of patients. Hustling our uncle into it, Laura tapes his mouth shut and trusses his hands. This is as about as much as I have ever been able to reconstruct the events of that day. When the robbery takes place my uncle is well over sixty; he had been late to start his medical career, entering medical school after his honorable discharge from the United States Army with the rank of captain. I do not now and will probably never know my sister's motives, though I have experimented over the years with theories, imagining the crime as a possible outgrowth of her increasingly irrational politics, radically left for a time and then—in the way of certain disaffected 1960s idealists— veering from one ideology to the next until finally she drifts into the lawless realm where the types that attract mixed-up former rich kids are by no means working out moral or ethical quandaries. They are criminals.

It is possible, of course, that drugs are involved; about this I am also unclear. What cannot be contested is that Laura's youthful act will trigger a sequence of detonations whose repercussions ripple through the whole of her life and mine and those of our parents and siblings and also eventually her own children. Her first daughter is an infant at the time of the robbery; eventually Laura will give birth to three more, two boys and a girl. Sometimes I think about these people I have never met and wonder where in our bloodlines this all began and when, if ever, it ends.

The truth is not knowable. I have thought over the years about transgenerational trauma. I have thought about genetic predisposition. I have thought about how misfortune can ripple fatefully through bloodlines. But those concepts do little to advance what seems to me the one irresistible conclusion: humans get hurt and hurt others in turn.

A writer friend, now dead, made the claim in a memoir that his father had, during his childhood, slipped into his bed after a drunken party and penetrated him. I do not doubt for a second my friend believed this awful violation took place. Neither am I saying it did not or could not have happened; no one would willingly cause further pain to victims of sexual abuse. Yet I also know that my friend—a charming and ornately neurotic fabulist and, not incidentally, recovering drug addict and alcoholic—was inclined in all ways to cut emotional corners. In a sense, there was some convenience for him, both emotionally and professionally, in tracing the origins of every fault line in his messy existence to a single horrific event. It was as if, by finding the crack in the foundation of what his siblings believed was a relatively happy childhood, by singling out the corrupt element, he could somehow excise it. Instead, he brought the house down on his head.

Despite the skepticism of some critics, the book was resoundingly praised. His siblings, naturally, were devastated by revelations impossible by then either to investigate or to refute, both parents having already died. In that way the events of that one drunken cocktail party in the 1950s were reinscribed. The damage continued to cascade.

Sometimes, when I am thinking about Laura, I like to recall nonsense verbal games we shared into early adulthood, sibling patter, strings of secret nonsense words, random snippets of dialogue we liked to quote from a bloated Panavision war epic we once had watched on TV. For years, instead of hello, when Laura lifted a telephone receiver, I would say "Gavabutu."

Gavabutu was a place name croaked, in his four-pack-a-day growl, by John Wayne playing Rear Admiral Rockwell Torrey in Otto Preminger's war epic *In Harm's Way*.

"Levu-Vana," Laura replied, Levu-Vana being the name of Gavabutu's sister island.

With that the conversation could begin.

Levu-Vana and Gavabutu are fictitious places, screenwriter substitutes for certain real islands where, over the course of the Pacific War, nearly thirty million very real human lives were lost. The geographies conjured in our nonsense exchange never existed, any more than there had ever been a strongbox of cash in my uncle's cellar, as my sister thought. That was what she'd gone to Babylon searching for, a stash. Given that my uncle was a hardscrabble survivor of the Great Depression, it was not the most far-fetched notion. Still, it was a child's scheme, a hunt for hidden treasure.

Whether she wanted the money to fund a commune or to buy a brick of coke or more guns, I'm not sure, nor even how much she imagined she might score. I doubt it was more than what it costs me to get her out of jail, money forfeited almost immediately because Laura, as will be seen, jumps bail.

The house in which these relatives lived with their only child, a son, was a shingled white Colonial. The side occupied by the family was notionally separated from where the medical practice was located past a pair of curtained French doors. There were four bedrooms and a bath upstairs, and if I knew the house well it is because these people—my father's second sister and her husband—frequently invited me to serve as a kind of companion for their lonely and friendless son.

My cousin was three years younger than I. Three years is an eternity when you are eight or nine. It was, in any case, a mismatched pairing, one I went along with out of general good-boy compliance and also because their dreary, staid household nevertheless offered escape from so much that felt unstable in my own, where I spent almost all my time burrowing into books in the bedroom, avoiding my pesky siblings and alarmed by my mother's increasing reliance on tranquilizers and white wine to fill the spaces where my often-absent father should have been.

Initially the job was passed off as babysitting. Since my cousin and I had little in common and he spent much of the time in his toy-filled bedroom, I floated around idly, irrelevant, eavesdropping on the doings in the doctor's office where my briskly efficient aunt frequently filled in for the receptionist. My cousin and I disliked each other equally. To me he was a spoiled little asshole. As he made clear, both his parents and he viewed me with a blend of suspicion and distaste. None of them bothers to conceal their disapproval of my family of strivers for having overreached what they see as our station.

Still, it fascinated me to watch this grim couple going through their days. Full of cheery, reassuring professionalism when seeing patients, they fell into cold silence as soon as they passed through those French doors.

At my relatives' house there were two zones of existence, and each was also sharply demarcated by smell: the private side sour with the tang of percolator coffee, the sterile, public one marked by the the sharp musty odors of rubbing alcohol. My unpaid companionship did come with inducements. There were Friday-night suppers at waterfront seafood restaurants with plastic-covered menus, French bread stained with melted butter, shrimp cocktails in martini glasses, even shopping trips to Best & Co. on the Miracle Mile in Manhasset. There—after my cousin had been fitted for kiddie blazers and neat gray flannel trousers and velveteen-collared Chesterfields—my aunt sometimes rewarded me with a pair of socks. There were outings to the great kiddie emporium FAO Schwarz in Manhattan, where my cousin was plied with toys and, from time to time, I was fobbed off with things like Chinese linking rings, classics of illusion magic whose special properties defeated me.

Though I cannot know what motivated Laura to hatch her weird scheme, I have sometimes envisioned the scene of her exiting the car, walking purposely across leafy Smith Street and through a privet hedge into a yard planted with blue hydrangeas. I can see her entering through a front office door habitually left unlocked. My aunt and cousin, as I understand, were away that day, although it is not clear how Laura could have known this or even whether this sort of intelligence even factored into her plan. The idea was to make off with the cash that many doctors then took in payment and some, like my uncle, did not declare. ("Better us than the IRS," as my aunt said.) And in my imagination of how this scene was meant to play out, Laura slips down the back stairs to the basement after tying up my uncle, grabs the fabled lockbox, and makes her getaway.

I could always, of course, have told her that there was no lockbox. I'd snooped around that basement enough to know as much and was also alert to the frequency of my aunt's trips to the bank to deposit money in my cousin's savings account. For me to have tipped off Laura would have required advance knowledge of her scheme. Since I'd had none, I was as dumbfounded as anyone by her audacity and devastated when other relatives made clear their assumption that we had been in cahoots.

Somehow my uncle got his hands free of the bonds. Somehow Laura managed for a short time to stay on the lam. She was caught soon enough, however, and arrested, presumably on the basis of a tip from someone who spied the suspicious license plates. Not long afterward my uncle died of the heart disease that ran as powerfully in his family as alcoholism. Having avoided the second curse, he could not escape the first and was buried just over a year after Laura was arraigned and sent to Riverhead county jail, her bail set at $10,000, which, as noted, I paid. Even before a trial date was set, there was a general familial verdict of guilt handed down on us both for delivering such a terrible shock to my uncle that it was thought to have killed him. In a sense, I guess it did.

While I don't want to get too far ahead of this story, it is worth saying here that during that long year before Laura stuck up our uncle, my father lost the last remaining shreds of Hawaiian Surf—after the bankruptcy filing necessitated by his partner's embezzlement scheme, he also lost the rights to the name—and then, more consequentially, my mother died. Without much noticing it, I begin to take on family responsibilities that she had always shouldered, and so it was I who was left scrambling—as best a barely employed twenty-two-year-old could—to find a defense attorney for Laura.

For quite a long time I could not fathom what the writer E. B. White meant when he referred to "the gift of loneliness and the gift of privacy" as the "queer prizes" New York bestows on those who desire them. Eventually I will, though; over time, the anonymous sanctuary of my city becomes very familiar to me, particularly that most public of civic spaces, Central Park. Intended by its designers as a sanctuary, it has been that to me—especially the less populated parts above Ninety-Sixth Street—and it is there I've been drawn in times of trouble for the simple and yet still surprising reason that it does bestow upon the lonely that queer prize of privacy.

At various times I have taken to the paths of the North Woods to wail in grief; have found myself the loneliest human on earth surrounded by thousands of people on a hot summer day at Lasker Pool; have puzzled out knotty problems while hiking a hill to the little-known fortress of the Blockhouse with my dog.

And, on a mild afternoon that will turn out to be the last time I see her for decades, I lie on the lawn of the Conservatory Garden with my sister Laura, blowing through grass whistles and planning a strategy to keep her out of prison. Conservatory Garden is an anomalous place in the context of the park, an invader shoehorned into the artificially rusticated nineteenth-century landscape envisioned by Frederick Law Olmsted and Calvert Vaux by the so-called master builder Robert Moses in the twentieth. I love it, though, with its deep green hedges of clipped yew, its crabapple allees so densely shady they cast you almost into darkness, its jetting fountain and wisteria-draped pergola, all entered through a pair of ornate ironwork gates that at one time graced the forecourt of the grandest of Long Island's Gilded Age mansions. The garden is reminiscent of the vacant North Shore estates where, not all that long ago, Laura and I and our hippie pals danced and rampaged and smoked weed and tripped out on acid.

Today more than most days I wish we could go back to all that. Yet it's plainly too late. Instead, we are soberly discussing attorneys and "options" and possible plea deals and plans that, sadly, only one of us understands to be a deception. This afternoon when we part, Laura will board the M4 bus down Fifth to Penn Station and then a commuter train to Mineola, where she is staying with a friend while awaiting arraignment. We will hug and say the empty things people say at moments like this, and whatever we say is meaningless because Laura already has plotted another course. Tomorrow or the next day she will meet her boyfriend—who may or may not, in fact, be her husband—and bundle their daughter into a car. Then she will vanish from sight for the next twenty years. Laura, I know now, never had any intention of sticking around.

During the years that follow, my sister will become a wanted person not unlike those in the post office flyers I tracked in childhood. I will also become a person of substantial ongoing interest to officials at the Federal Bureau of Investigation. Like my relatives, the feds assumed I had been in on the scheme. And while my relatives settle for shunning me, the FBI takes a more aggressive stance, summoning me regularly to headquarters for what they term "conversations," keeping my little studio apartment under surveillance and bugging my land-line. Throughout these years I will mentally revisit that scene in the park and question everything I failed or refused to see. How did the wild and lovable, smart and impetuous, fearless younger sister I tried all my life to protect become a stranger? Could the person who held me so tight that day that I could feel her heart fluttering through her rib cage be the stranger who planted a Judas kiss? Had I been asking myself the wrong questions all along? In taking off for life underground, was Laura not following our mother's childhood advice about riptides? The currents of her life were too forceful to resist. Perhaps she imagined it was better to let fate carry her away until it was safe to come ashore.

For twenty years, I will not hear another word from or about Laura, not until she slips up somehow after years of hiding and the FBI finds and arrests her. Living on a farm in a rural corner of southern Ohio not far from the Kentucky border, she is extradited to New York to face trial. By this time she has four children, has lived under a series of aliases, and held a variety of largely menial jobs using assumed identities. To some degree, despite the obvious persistent paranoia of being hunted, her life as I understand it is somehow stable. That ends when she is extradited to New York, tried and con-victed on the old charges, and sent to prison. But that is a story to save for later.

Somehow, and parallel to this and every other turn of events in the year before I turn twenty-three, I begin to find my way. Fortune is, as usual, the dominant force. How else to make sense of the way that years spent hanging around creative odd-balls, drugged-up drag queens with washed-up Hollywood characters and the Warhol-adjacent, will turn out to have been enough education to enter any kind of profession, let alone one I have never for one second considered pursuing?

Journalism comes into my life by way of Jamaica Kincaid, who has ditched her trade journal job for freelance work at magazines and alternative weeklies, mostly writing eccentric personal essays on such topics as how the world might be improved if it were run by mammies (that is meant literally: one article was titled "If Mammies Ruled the World"). Figuring I might as well give writing a crack, I telephone Rosemary Kent, a woman who, as accessories editor at *Women's Wear Daily,* often featured Frying Pan Ranch designs in the pages of that industry rag. Somehow because she knows Andy Warhol, and because he's realized that his fledgling magazine needs at least some trained professionals, she has been hired as editor in chief of *Interview.*

"I always knew there was more to you than making tchotchkes," she says when I visit her at the *Interview* offices, a disarmingly bland space some floors below the Union Square "Factory," which is exotically furnished with flea market finds bought cheaply in Paris and overseen by a stuffed Great Dane called Cecil.

I feel like a fraud, of course, when I take on my first assignments, like one of the parody primitives bumbling into a civilized clearing (a croquet game, in fact) in George W. S. Trow's movie *Savages,* initially suspicious of this tribe that seems willing to take me in. This feeling hangs on for a long while, accompanying it a nagging terror that my near-total lack of formal schooling will be found out. Yet, as it happens, this presents no particular problem now or ever.

Never in my life will I compose a résumé. What would there be to record? "Summary of objectives"? None. "Education"? Negligible. "Hard skills"? Sixth-grade French, how to mix a speedball (recipe courtesy of Jackie Curtis), and how to drive a school bus. This last is no incidental competence. During the first days of "reporting" for *Interview,* I have taken and passed the test for an "S" level CDL driver's license, which entitles me to drive commercial vehicles. Between assignments I supplement the $25 article fees by commuting to Long Island to drive suburban school bus routes that leave from a depot in Huntington and loop from Centerport to Northport. "Additional skills"? Can parallel park anything on up to six wheels.

And, yes, of course there was the parade of odd jobs: grunt at Max's Kansas City, illustrator's model, disco juice boy, along with a brief stint as a salesclerk in a rich-hippie cobbler shop on West Eleventh Street, where I once sold some lace-up boots to Jimi Hendrix, who promptly returned them. There was the episode of the buckskin bags and then the kitschy bijoux, successful enough in an enterprising way yet hardly an inducement to employ me.

Already by then most grad schools had developed journalism programs; it would not be long before advanced degrees were required to get a gig as an unpaid intern. It should be said that my news judgment was also notional, my article pitches based mostly on random enthusiasms. Nevertheless it was possible for an amateur like me, lacking the least concept of what constituted an inverted pyramid structure or a nut paragraph, to vamp his way through writing profiles of Don Murray, a genial actor who once played opposite Marilyn Monroe in *Bus Stop;* or of the Chilean heiress who oversaw the press affairs of

Yves Saint Laurent (and who also, although I was too ignorant at the time to know it, was instrumental to Rudolf Nureyev's defection from the Soviet Union to France); and of Earl Blackwell, an oily character who for decades operated the Celebrity Register, a subscription hybrid of the Social Register and the White Pages. I wrote about the expatriate English author (and icon of gay liberation) Christopher Isherwood, who during our interview stubbornly deferred half the questions to his far younger boyfriend, the artist Don Bachardy, with the result that the reader was left with little insight about either of them.

Out of either stubbornness or pretention I resisted as too idiotic the Q-and-A interviews that were the magazine's bread and butter. Even with zero skills I knew I was better than that.

After a year of this I had advanced very little. More to the point, I had not found myself miraculously swept up into Andy Warhol's glamorous coterie, as I yearned to be. I did somehow befriend the socialite photographer Peter Beard—still at the peak of his WASP glamour and beauty and not yet a coke-addled and self-mythologizing mess—through his then girlfriend, Barbara Allen, a lissome Air Force brat from New Mexico who had beautiful legs and a voice that was a gorgeous, husky purr. Barbara, a sometime model and gold digger, was the ex-wife of a pulp paper heir who was among the publication's financial backers. When we met she was introduced to me as the "back issues" clerk, which, given that monthly magazine had been in existence for under five years, cannot have been a terribly strenuous job.

In some manner I can no longer reliably identify, I had come to know the artist Ray Johnson, the founder of the

"School of Correspondence" art, an extravagantly gifted loner whose life will overlap with mine over the decades in eerily fateful ways. Ray and I exchanged countless letters, sending each other mail "art" consisting of just about anything that fit in an envelope. Sometimes these were collages. Sometimes they were newspaper clippings. Sometimes they were exquisite corpse-type chain mail with emendations added by other "correspondents" along the line. Occasionally I sent Ray images made with a transfer process Peter Beard taught me that required rubbing magazine pages with gasoline-soaked rags. Ray sent back lists, and lists of lists, mad taxonomies being one of his specialties.

Though Ray could hardly get arrested in the art world in those early days, the lists later formed a cornerstone of what curators and collectors referred to as his "oeuvre." Written in distinctive type and often ornamented with faux-naive drawings, the lists were of art-world personages or movie stars or secretly gay movie stars or anything else that crossed the mind of this obsessive creature who lived in a small frame house very far from SoHo or any other art-world nexus in suburban Locust Valley.

Among my favorites was Ray's *Laundry List,* with its itemization of laundry services from Madame Bellas to American Flag Hand Laundry, Blue Bird Laundry, and Jung Young Wetwash Co. Inc. But I am also fond of his *Famous People's Mother's Potato Mashers,* with its images of S-shaped, perforated wire-mesh mashers purportedly inspired by those in the kitchen drawers of people like, say, Alexandra Anderson, the arts editor at *The Village Voice.*

It sounds ludicrous to propose that one's professional vocation began in earnest with Alexandra Anderson's mother's potato masher, but such is the case. Founded in 1955 by Dan Wolf, Edwin Fancher, John Wilcock, and Norman Mailer as an alternative newsweekly situated to the political left—although often by not much—of mainstream organs like *The New York Times* and the daily tabloids, the *Voice* at this point was nearing its apogee in terms of circulation, reputation, critical sway, and, most important, advertising revenue. The *Voice* would eventually cease print publication in 2017 before being feebly revived in the years that followed, yet never again would it regain the physical heft and cultural status it enjoyed in the years when New York still supported a booming counterculture, in the days before Craigslist and the rest of the internet came along to divert and then swallow whole the deluge of revenue represented by thousands of lucrative classified ads.

Set by hand each week in tiny agate type, these ads were sorted in columns offering Instruction, Winter Shares, Summer Shares, Entertainment, Professional Services, Help Wanted, Rides to Share, Merchandise, Where to Find It, Situations Wanted, Answering Services, Escort Services, Personals, and also a miscellaneous category dedicated to entreaties to Saint Jude, the patron saint of lost or desperate causes. In later years, these perplexing ads were said to have been coded communiqués sent by operatives of the Irish Republican Army.

Owing to all the ad revenue (quarterly profits of the *Voice* were $255,000 in 1974, the equivalent of about $1.5 million today), the weekly paper was thick as a doormat. The more ads, the more editorial pages that needed filling and, naturally, the more opportunity to showcase articles that, as *The*

New York Times once condescendingly noted, evolved in a "sharper" and "more professional" direction than those in the paper's early, Mailer days, better defined and edited, less likely to "meander like a muddy river." The *Voice* cost twenty-five cents at the time and came out on Wednesdays. It was so vital a source of real estate listings that a queue of apartment hunters formed at dawn outside a specific newsstand on Sheridan Square, where the earliest issues were heaved off the back of a truck.

Recollection here, while hazy, suggests that it was through Vince Aletti, an epistolary aquaintance met on the grapevine of Ray Johnson's chain letters (and who will go on to become a lifelong friend), that I learn Alexandra—everyone calls her Ally—Anderson needs an assistant. Ray himself mentions that, at a certain point in her past, Ally herself worked as an assistant to the artist Joseph Cornell, as though this were required information. It will turn out to be true and also the case that, while Ally seldom says much about the quirky bachelor who lives in a homely frame structure in Queens with his mother and disabled brother, he does make a present to her of several of his coveted shadowbox artworks.

This is not altogether surprising given that Ally is a bright, WASPy society blonde who was, in her youth, as lissome as the ballet-dancer types Cornell idolized. The job as Cornell's helper was in a roundabout way Ally's ticket into a closed, chummy art world then on the verge of exploding; somehow, she had parlayed the lowly assistant job into a thriving career as an art writer, more enthusiast than critic, and eventually a connector who seemed to know everyone. That full-access pass to both the grungy downtown arts sphere the *Voice* had traditionally covered and the uptown gallery scene only just beginning to grow into what will become known as the arts industrial complex brought her to the attention of the *Voice*'s new boss, a publishing wunderkind named Clay Felker. He saw in Ally a kind of twofer. She had skills and connections. Just as important to the advertising potential that increased arts coverage represented, she had few enemies, something you could not say of many on the *Voice*'s editorial staff.

I call on a Monday. Ally immediately invites me to her office. "When did you have in mind?"

"This afternoon?"

Swapping shifts with a fellow bus driver, I race into Manhattan from Long Island and hoof it from Penn Station to the *Voice* headquarters, a five-story stucco shoebox on Eleventh Street and University Place. The front-desk clerk at the time may or may not have been the future critic James Wolcott. Memory here is fuzzy. Whoever it is directs me to the fourth floor and instructs me to find an office at the end of a long hall.

If the *Interview* offices were intentionally designed to produce a vaguely corporate aura, the *Voice* is exactly the kind of bohemian-hive cartoon you'd expect. A five-story stack of funky cubicles laid out along the long window walls of this anonymous rectangular building, it has windows on two sides, a network of narrow corridors and shared unisex bathrooms with perennially balky plumbing. At the very end of the fourth floor, facing directly into the tree canopy on Eleventh Street and over a row of genteel if run-down nineteenth-century townhouses—multimillion-dollar real estate is a thing of the future—is a cramped office divided down the middle by a windowed partition. On one side sits a desk and several filing cabinets covered by a sprawl of publicity photographs, catalogs, books, invitations, gallery announcements, and listing stacks of yellow typing paper. On the other is the neatly organized sturdy Metalcraft desk of the man whose Sisyphean weekly job it is to compile and input by typewriter the free listings.

To reach Ally's office you must first pass the partially closed door of another one, from which emanates a trail of weed smoke. Somewhere inside are the paper's two perennially stoned "Scenes" reporters, who between them compile lurid, if irresistible, first-person dispatches from a constant round of nightlife adventures: singles parties, swinger clubs, discos, and "happenings" like the Stonewall riots, during which one of the reporters somehow manages to get pinned inside the bar.

Ally's office is vacant, so I clear off a desk chair and take a seat with my back to the window. An hour passes and then another as I survey the tumult—blue Bics launched in every direction, slumping boxes of art-world flyers, tilted mailing tubes, and piles of glossy photographs scattered like loose scree. Tentatively at first but then with growing determination I begin to neaten up. Working in from the perimeter, I start by sorting the photos, categorizing and organizing them into somewhat arbitrary groupings: Art-world personages like Cy Twombly, Robert Rauschenberg, Merce Cunningham, John Cage, and Robert Wilson go in one stack, Charles Ludlam, Sam Shepard, Meredith Monk in another. W. H. Auden and Louise Bogan join a much smaller selection of images rubber-stamped on the reverse side "The American Academy of Poets." It had not pre-

Ray Johnson, from a prophetic 1980s photo series
titled Ray Johnson, Bound & Drowned

Alexandra Anderson, 1977

viously occurred to me that poets had head shots. Martha Graham is a category unto herself, so numerous are the pictures of her striking mythical freeze-tag poses.

When I'm finished with this, I gather up all the pens and, sorting the leaking dead ones from those with working nibs, then start to sort the mailing tubes, thinking little about where I get the nerve to invade this landfill belonging to a complete stranger. It's a risky move and possibly misguided. Certainly it is compulsive, but then this is a function of my jitters and a habit of industry I inherited from my mom. I am also inspired by the amazing stuff I come upon. Tucked into a box that once held mimeograph paper are original black-and-white proof prints from a photo-essay the great Magnum photographer W. Eugene Smith made of an industrial disaster at Minamata, Japan. How they've come to be here I'm not sure yet. Eventually I will understand that in this predigital world photographers frequently submit photographic prints for publication, often ones they have developed in their own darkrooms.

Horrific and simultaneously tender and moving, the photos document the industrial disaster that started in the 1930s, when methylmercury was dumped by a local chemical factory, along with industrial wastewater, into Minamata Bay. From there it spread to the Shiranui Sea. The heavy metals contained in the water poisoned fish and shellfish and eventually everything up the length of the food chain including, of course, humans. Children exposed to the toxins developed neurological disorders that crippled and deformed them. Though their grotesquely torqued bodies resemble figures from Goya's hell, the horror is tempered somewhat by the compassion Smith captured in the faces of parents and guardians who cradled and bathed and attempted to give the victims nourishment. The photos are publicity images from a gallery show. It says so on the back of each. By now I have stopped looking at the pictures themselves and am engrossed instead in the captions Scotch-taped to the images—in particular one whose abbreviated legend notes that mercury brought on fatal brain seizures in felines whose onset was termed "dancing cat fever." I am trying to picture this when my potential future employer breezes through the door in a swirl of cashmere scarves and tote bags and plops into a chair.

Ally Anderson glances around with an expression that suggests awareness of things looking different. She asks about references though not qualifications and mentions that the job is as an assistant editor. Some writing may be involved. She does not specify what sort of pay is involved or terms. Twenty minutes into the interview, if that's what this is, she startles me by asking when I can start.

This is a Monday; I begin work the next week, in the bicentennial summer of 1976. Within the first month I have finished tidying the office; officiously devised a photo filing system; started to grasp the rudiments of text editing, which will continue to be done on paper for some years to come. I quickly learn basic proofreading hieroglyphics and the meaning of "dele" and "stet."

Much of the work involves editing a weekly critical guide to the city's cultural highlights, pithy snippets that for the writers who produce them are primarily money spinners to boost their meager paychecks. "They are not for the collected works," as the novelist and essayist Blanche McCrary Boyd says.

However, for the artists, dancers, photographers, film-makers, writers, poets, videographers, singers, and assorted performance artists who have thronged a run-down metropolis where rents are dirt cheap and talent is prime cultural capital, the listings are a lifeline. Relative to the myriad ways technology will one day make possible the rocket trip from obscurity to fame in hours or minutes, the *Voice* listings may seem as efficient as smoke signals. Yet during this ancient epoch in the predigital mists of 1975 they are, essentially, Instagram, Twitter, and TikTok rolled into one.

Decades later at a *Voice* reunion, I run into Edwin Fancher, one of the paper's founders, bearded and frail at ninety-four, though peppery still. I introduce myself and remark to him how surprising it is to me that I'd been offered a job at the *Voice* despite my lack of experience, education, or even a résumé. "Oh, we didn't hire anyone who had a journalism degree back then," he flatly replies.

When I join its staff, the paper has recently changed hands, purchased by a handful of wealthy Ivy League patricians. There is no apparent reason why this group of trust-funded socialite clubmen might wish to invest in a "commie pinko rag" peopled by an unruly assortment of rabble-rousing lefties, brainy feminists, muckrakers of varied political persuasions, a smattering of black intellectuals and Jewish intellectuals, and one at first and then, when another comes out of the closet, two gay reporters, as well as a lesbian dance critic whose diaristic columns are composed in epic sentences running on for paragraphs.

A great deal of these people's energy and time, it seems, will be taken up with feuding in print or in the newspaper's offices, where the physical layout is demarcated less according to function than factionalism. There is an influential music section overseen by a gruff windbag who positions himself as the solar center of a constellation of rock music fanboys, Dylan exegetes, Hunter Thompson wannabes, few if any women, and the occasional gay writer who appears in its pages as if on a special visa. By and large the place is chockablock with such outsize personalities, people with egos the size of parade floats, and this suits me. I find I can camouflage myself unobtrusively in the shadow of these characters while quietly sussing things out. Though the gig has no real job description, I pick up editing quickly enough and learn how to massage the free-form prose of the contributors into some kind of sense.

Writing is the one aspect of the new job where I can objectively be said to show some native ability, yet I do little of it at first, mostly spending my time tidying up snippets submitted by an arts staff given to prose occasionally so parodically high-flown it seems like material for a stand-up routine.

When, in a squib about a Sam Shepard play, the chief theater critic blasts "the mephitic fake naturalism of his dramaturgy," I conclude that the sanest approach is to back away from the sentence gently. When the newspaper's chief photographer and self-appointed photo critic submits some sub-literate copy, I take a more helpful, hands-on approach and am startled when this does not meet with his immediate approval. I recognize now that, while people say the way to learn writing is to read the work of one's betters, much can be said of bad writing as a tool of instruction. There are fewer seductions, and the pitfalls are easier to detect. Besides, it is never in short supply.

"What do you think you're doing, you arrogant little prick?" the critic says, bodily bearing down on me in my desk chair. "If you ever change a comma of mine again, I'll throw you out the window."

Nonetheless, I carry on whittling away at his wooden critiques and then, soon enough, with no one to object, make forays of my own into crafting written snippets and recommendations, unimpeded by ignorance and a bit giddy with the newfound pleasure of composing paragraphs that will magically lead to the typositor room. If I still don't know how I plan to fit into the wider world, I now have the very real existential affirmation of a byline. It's right there, in print on a regular basis, plump black-and-white characters spelling out my name in bold-condensed Times Roman.

Soon summer rolls around and, with it, Ally's abrupt announcement of plans to decamp for a month to her farmhouse in coastal Maine. "Don't worry, you'll be fine, dear," she says chipperly before handing off all editorial duties. She disappears, and I settle in assuming she knows something about me that I don't.

Within the year the rote critics' recommendations begin to evolve along with me, and the section I'm putting together more and more on my own develops a different tone, quirky and playful, adventurous in a way that mirrors so much of what is currently going on in the city. Like a grown-up version of the activities page in the kiddie magazine *Highlights,* the double-truck centerfold becomes a playground for untried talents spotted by me or sent my way, people like the cartoonists Roz Chast, Mark Alan Stamaty, Stan Mack, Lynda Barry, and Walter Gurbo; the photographers Robert Mapplethorpe, Arlene Gottfried, and Peter Hujar; the humorists Cynthia Heimel and Warren Leight; the biographer C. Carr; the essayists Mim Udovitch and Lisa Kennedy; and a raft of poets and critics and novelists who will include Colson Whitehead, Lisa Jones, Nelson George, Brian Parks, Greg Tate, Hilton Als, and others who, obscure at the time, will eventually occupy their rightful place at the center of the broader culture.

Looking back, I see that there is something about the broke and crippled city that makes it hospitable to talent, something beyond the obvious explanation that rents are cheap. Some shreds of postsixties idealism are still part of the atmosphere. Passion is a currency. So is the raw talent that, for now, seems enough to get a foot in most doors. A friend put it this way: "If you claimed you were something when I first came to the city, people never questioned it," he said, referring to the seventies, when nobody had ever met an investment banker but everyone knew painters and writers and illustrators and directors and radically engaging performance artists like Karen Finley, whose career seems impossible to conceive of happening now, or somebody who was starting up a band. "They just said, 'Show me.'"

Thus the pasty, moody, and unprepossessing young telephone receptionist at the *Voice* will soon enough become a vaunted culture critic celebrated for verbal fireworks. The shy copy editor with one cast eye will emerge as what a critic later deems "the modern Jewish Jane Austen." The goofy punk boy in the messenger room, the skinny one with Coke-bottle eye-glasses, will amass first underground renown as a No Wave bandleader and then much broader fame as an influential music producer.

Dorothy Reed and Mary Wright are the *Voice*'s equable receptionists, and it is not exactly to the paper's credit that theirs will remain among the only black faces on staff until affirmative action initiatives forcefully direct management toward increased diversity. My spot in the editorial hierarchy is barely a half step above the clerical, yet I'm happy to occupy it and to have a regular perch in the mouse-infested cubbyhole we occupy at the end of a warren of offices that have the aura of a diorama from the Museum of Weird.

I picture taking a tour group through here and pointing out the oddities: here we have the bearded, briarwood smoking grump of a columnist who spent decades burrowing into the First Amendment, lost in a lair with a vast wooden desk buried in papers dusted with pipe ash; here the even more disordered cubicle of the great feminist thinker, a woman of such elevated cast of mind her thoughts must arise like a lotus from the muck; and here the lava-lighted lair of the two Scenes columnists, its bookshelves sagging beneath the weight of novelty gizmos, skateboards, inflatable sex dolls, leather harnesses, dildos, and fleshlights that are regularly sent to them for "review."

Our own cramped space is, as mentioned, divided in half. We share it with Listings. Essentially this department consists of one editor and a part-time assistant, the two of them stationed across from us, visible through a windowed pass-through. Unacknowledged by anyone, this duo runs what is in some way the newspaper's nerve center. While few on staff spare a thought for Listings, it is likely the section that the greatest number of New Yorkers consult. The man who runs it is a rumpled, noncerebral type who carries in his head a Venn diagram of downtown culture. Prospecting through the slipstream of daily listings submissions in this prehistoric, pre-internet era, it is he, with his quirky sensibility, who is an important decider. It is he who judges which storied jazz wizard or which new performance artist will feature in the listings, which Judson Theatre warhorse giving a reading cannot be missed. For the 150 people passionate about these things, he is the messenger giving the secret location of a downtown building where a legendary Japanese butoh dancer will mime his own death by hanging upside down from the cornice by a rope.

In what little spare time he has, this editor also edits a column called "Kids" and when in future decades I encounter, as adults, people whose bohemian household reading included *The Village Voice,* they often confirm what I always suspected: Kids never read the Kids column. Who would, when readers of any age could feast on a cornucopia of bizarre happenings throughout the city, let alone the escort and dominatrix ads, the cryptic lovelorn ads at the back of the book: "Cer, All knees, no brains, you don't need her. T," or "David, I need You, Please get in touch, Agnes in Chicago," or "Snarf Narfleson You're The Greatest I Love You"? Who could fail to love Snarf Narfleson?

Lou Reed said you always need a fallback. Touch-typing

was his. And, as it happens, the sullen rock god was far from alone in having acquired his handy vocational-school skill, a fact I learn by observing a revolving cast of temp typists that pass through the Listings office next door, over time among them a future Tony Award–winning composer, a future Obie-winning playwright, a future Emmy-winning screenwriter, a future Grammy-winning luminary on the alternative music scene, and an enigmatic ghost-pale goth chick with raven black hair, armloads of inking, and a cello she hauls around in what looks like a kiddie coffin.

Julia Kent lasts longer than most any assistant, yet eventually she quits, too, to follow her training as a classically skilled experimental musician who gains a following, records and tours with Antony (later Anohni) and the Johnsons and her own group, Rasputina, writes somber orchestra compositions played across Europe, and achieves her own niche fame. For the time being, she is a drudge like the rest of us, akin to those creatures in the "Hidden Picture" features in the Sunday papers. You'd have to scour the landscape to find us, representatives of a stubborn breed the actress Ruth Gordon once characterized as "stupid dreamers," concealed in the cultural shrubbery, indisputably there.

At some point early in these days, I come to the attention of a generous-minded editor who, feeling the paper needs more profiles, encourages me to try my hand at writing a column. Initially she is interested in word snapshots of whoever happens to be making some cultural news at the time, and there are no shortage of those: Talking Heads, the punk girl group Bush Tetras, a new singer called Madonna. I write some, but these people interest me less than characters nobody else seems to take much note of, types any of us have passed without learning more about as we bumble through the city, its odd-balls and anomalies, its holdouts, the obsessives and those rare birds, the die-hard utopians.

Because there is no template at the *Voice* for this column, we settle on a thousand-word weekly exploration of the city, a column whose roots, the way I see it, are traceable to *Wild Kingdom,* a nature show I watched as a kid. Sponsored by the insurance giant Mutual of Omaha, *Wild Kingdom* featured a zoologist, Marlin Perkins—handsome, avuncular, with a white pencil mustache; a reedy, animal-friendly voice pitched soothingly low; and an evident love of his subject. Each week Perkins ventured out to explore wild creatures in their habitats, accompanied by his suspiciously handsome assistant, Jim Fowler.

The person assigned to shoot pictures for the column is Sylvia Plachy, a picture researcher only recently promoted to staff photographer. While over the next two decades the two of us will form a partnership that frames our working lives, our biographies could not be more unalike. A Hungarian émigré ten years my senior, Sylvia came to the US as a teenager fleeing the anti-Stalinist 1956 revolution, her family's escape plotted in secret and carried out on a single afternoon. Such was the danger of leaving that Sylvia was given little time to pack and none to bid her friends goodbye. Conspirators drove the family—Sylvia and her parents—to a farmstead deep in the countryside, where they were hustled into the bed of a horse cart and covered with a layer of freshly harvested corn.

Once past a variety of checkpoints, they were deposited at the edge of a wood and told to run for the border, to be met by Red Cross workers who gave them each a Hershey bar and an orange. Thus began a hegira that would see them bedding down in refugee camps, the apartments of distant relatives, and Viennese SRO hotels as they navigated a morass of visa quotas, their ultimate goal immigration to the US.

Eventually, two years after their escape from Budapest, they arrived on American shores on a stifling August day, their port of debarkation Idlewild Airport. Busing from there to Grand Central Terminal, they continued onward to Union City, where an aunt of Sylvia's mother had agreed to sponsor and take in her small family. To extend the train of improbability, Sylvia's parents went on to give their shy, dreamy daughter a proper American secondary education—despite strict Catholic school training she would never completely lose her Hungarian accent—and then propel her onward through art school at Pratt Institute. From there, by way of an encounter with Clay Felker—at the time a star editor at the *Herald Tribune*'s Sunday magazine—Sylvia found her way to the *Voice*. Like myself, she began there as a lowly assistant, a photo editor.

Out of this unlikely convergence of fates develops an enduring professional partnership that will last for two decades. During those years we will develop a working routine that entails heading out together either on foot or in one of her beat-up jalopies, venturing mostly by instinct or following random tips, into various corners of New York. Over time these wanderings will develop decipherable patterns, something in the mold of series TV, as we explore the city's many precincts, both aboveground and below, assembling an almost Proustian cast of characters as we venture to high places and low covering homicides, happenings, writers, street scenes, circus performances, and animals. Not infrequently we find ourselves in dodgy circumstances, places where we have no business being, and my theory about how we manage this is that, while neither of us can be characterized as especially adventurous or foolhardy, we share a nimbleness and an ability to adapt quickly to whatever life throws at us, possibly as a result of childhood or else because we are idiots.

Not surprisingly, we sometimes go wrong. I am thinking here of Crown Heights, Brooklyn, in the aftermath of an accident in which two children of Guyanese immigrants are struck, and one killed, when a car in a motorcade following a Hasidic grand rabbi, Menachem Mendel Schneerson, runs a red light.

Black radio in those days is all I listened to, and on the afternoon of the accident my radio was tuned to the R&B station WBLS, which reported the incident in a brief news spot and predicted the eruption of long-simmering local tensions. It will be almost twenty-four hours before the mainstream press moves in to cover what become the Crown Heights riots; by then Sylvia and I have filed our story and are gone. What I never mention in the report is how, as we canvased Kingston Avenue for community reaction, we were suddenly targeted and chased by an angry mob, sent running for our lives before ducking in desperation into a beauty salon, where a proprietor none too willingly pulled us inside and yanked down the riot gate.

I am thinking also of another kind of story we later pursued, this one in the desolate Romanian countryside, after the bloody overthrow of the dictator Nicolae Ceaușescu, where we traveled one bitter winter late in 1989, ill-prepared and uncredentialed, searching for a dissident Episcopal bishop who was also, as it happened, targeted by heavily armed rogue bands of the secret police, the Securitate.

The idea of reporting on foreign war zones, which had never entered my thoughts until this point, was not on my long list of life goals, to the extent that I had one. Sylvia and I remained then about equally astonished to be receiving regular paychecks and health benefits, each of us privately convinced we would eventually be found out by our employers as frauds. When impostor syndrome threatened, I tended then to recall a key lesson from my shoplifting days, a snippet of advice given to me by a speed freak I once met whose specialty was department-store theft. "Whatever it is, act as if you already own it," she said. "Never doubt yourself because the moment you hesitate you're fucked."

By then I had spent a decade and a half writing almost exclusively about the city. While I hadn't exhausted my subject matter, I was nagged by a remark made by a friend who was not much of a friend. "Don't you ever tire of the sidelong glance?" she asked, and the observation stung enough that I was inspired to approach the paper's new editor in chief and persuade him to assign me a story on the aftermath of the Romanian revolution. I imagined then that by writing about a conflict with complex geopolitical underpinnings—rather than the quirky delights of the "unexpected things" Robert

Rauschenberg once said awaited us all around every corner in New York—I could establish for myself some greater seriousness of purpose.

I had a leg up, since, having been in Budapest, Sylvia still spoke the language that dominated in the part of Romania where the revolution began. So, barely credentialed, on a shoestring budget, and in the days before cell phones existed, we flung ourselves headlong into an impossible situation. In retrospect it is clear we had zero business being in Romania, where, on Christmas Day, just hours after Ceauşescu was chased from his office, two Danish television journalists were killed on the outskirts of Bucharest and where shortly thereafter a *New York Times* correspondent was severely wounded when shots blasted through the side panel of his moving car. United Press International bulletins warned of armed Securitate agents roaming the region around Timişoara, a city that remained "the scene of some of the bloodiest massacres of civilians by Romanian security forces loyal to ousted President Nicolae Ceauşescu."

Undeterred, we two nobodies crossed the border in a car illegally rented in Budapest, plunged through a blanched winter landscape straight out of Turgenev, careering through the pitilessly cold countryside where, aside from the occasional horse cart driven by a fur-bundled lump barely distinguishable as human, the roads were vacant. Our plan was to track down the dissident Episcopal bishop who had dared to confront the brutal Ceauşescu and thus triggered the revolution.

Ceauşescu by now was already dead. He'd been captured on Christmas Day as he and his wife, Elena, made an abortive escape by helicopter from the roof of the Central Committee

Crown Heights riot, 1991
© Sylvia Plachy

building and then by road in a car said to have been weighed down by a cache of looted gold. You can easily Google their videotaped execution, which makes for satisfying viewing if you happen to believe in karma. It's a chaotic clip, full of orders barked by the dictator's captors, a kangaroo "trial," and their almost instantaneous conviction.

Given the unbridled horrors characteristic of Ceaușescu's nearly twenty-five-year rule—a feature of which was rampant torture and summary execution of opponents and onetime allies alike—there is little inducement to find humanity in the sad, imperious outbursts both Ceaușescus make in court. All the same you can identify with their desperation as the judges hastily exit the makeshift courtroom, soldiers truss the couple with what looks like laundry line, Nicolae clutches his hat, Elena fastens her fur collar, and they are herded into a courtyard where the camera delicately cuts away while on the soundtrack there is a sound like a stack of plates being dropped from a roof.

When the camera returns, two inert figures lie on the cold ground, their heads surrounded by pools of what looks like movie-prop blood.

We did, as it happened, find Bishop László Tőkés, tucked away in a safe house secreted in the Carpathian mountains. Snow there had fallen so deeply that streets were the width of a single shoveled footpath. We parked at the edge of a village, made our way to an onion-domed church, were ushered into a smoky rectory and served cucumber sandwiches on brown bread, and conducted what I suppose was an interview.

Looking back, I can't recollect how we managed this, given

that the entire security apparatus of the country and half the Western press corps were also looking for the same man. What matters is that I can also see quite clearly now how, for me, the interview had never been the point; the point was not, in fact, to prove my bona fides to my boss or my worth to a snide competitive friend but to escape my city, which had in recent years become a ghost-infested place.

Without being able at the time to articulate the feeling, I had grown soul-sick from attending memorial services, was hounded by rage at government inaction in confronting a deadly pandemic and by the way the suffering I saw all around me was greeted with contempt, not respect. And I was increasingly fearful that, with each corner I turned, I might suddenly find myself face-to-face with some half-dead friend. It happened often.

The last time I saw my photographer buddy Scott Heiser, the lymph glands in his neck had swollen so grotesquely that he was chinless. Although for a brief moment at the corner of Astor Place we tried making small talk, it was impossible; Scott's pupils were abnormally dilated, and his eyes darted about constantly like those of a trapped animal.

To look at any epidemiological bar graph charting mortality rates from acquired immune deficiency syndrome in the United States at the peak of the pandemic is to note a severe spike toward the final months of 1989. That figure on a graph was no abstraction to me, since large numbers of friends, acquaintances, and the subjects of my writing had died over the past decade, their numbers increasing sharply toward the end of the eighties. Between July 3, 1981, when a *New York Times* article reported on a "Rare Cancer Seen in 41 Homosexuals," and the peak of the pandemic in the United States, there would be 117,508 reported cases and 89,343 deaths, by a substantial percentage the majority of these in New York City. Buried alongside those dead men and women was the city in which I came of age.

Years ago a director I know shot a documentary in which he visited the last known addresses of certain of these people, or anyway the more celebrated among them, using images of private houses, apartment blocks, building numbers as emblems of a lost generation. It was, I suppose, his way of putting stones on their graves. Yet he must have been aware even as he was filming of how futile the undertaking was, how quickly the waters would close over that generational chapter, those deaths largely rendered a nonevent, one whose principal memorial is a vast quilt folded up in storage much of the time.

Though the film was draggy—in the way I imagine those Hollywood tours of houses where stars no one remembers once lived are bound to disappoint—I liked it because some of those people, like the performance artist and drag queen Ethyl Eichelberger, had been friends of mine. Still, the film's theme felt sententious, its underlying premise having been once made in a more profound and succinct way by a single sentence in Toni Cade Bambara's "The Education of a Storyteller" (published in a book whose title is *Deep Sightings and Rescue Missions*).

"What," Bambara wrote, "are we pretending not to know today?"

Back on the road to Timişoara, Sylvia and I stopped overnight at what had once been the grandest hotel in Cluj. It was an immense palatial pile on a hill surrounded by dense woods.

As elsewhere throughout the country, there was no electricity and certainly no heat. The room doors had no locks; Sylvia and I shared a single bed and were forced to wear all the clothes we had with us for warmth. Our documents and her photo equipment made a fence between us like a bundling board.

We slept as best we could and at dawn scrounged for tea in the lobby of the hotel, heading out just past daybreak along a mountain two-lane running parallel to a silvery river rimed with ice. Whiteness blanketed sky and blotted out the horizon, as though we were voyaging inside a snow globe. Suddenly, at a crossroads, we found ourselves being waved down by a group of soldiers, weapons drawn. There were four of them, all very young. Grunting, the lead soldier pointed to the trunk, which I keyed open while backing away toward a snowbank. First tossing our duffels and other possessions onto the road, the soldiers probed Sylvia's camera bags with the ends of their gun barrels, and from our exchanged glances emerged a clear, mutual understanding that it would be nothing for these men to shoot us and steal the car. Who would know?

Just then a soldier examining one of Sylvia's expensive Leica lenses dropped it. Instinctively she snapped at him in Hungarian. Startled and sheepish, he set down the bag and then minutes that lasted eternities passed before abruptly the soldiers got into their vehicle and drove off.

"What just happened?" I asked her.

"I have no idea," Sylvia replied.

In my early *Voice* days the colleague who ran the Listings department told me about a canoe trip he'd once made on the

Usumacinta River during the Guatemalan civil war. "You never know, in those situations, when you'll turn a corner and run into some retarded sixteen-year-old with a machine gun," he said.

He and some gay hippie friends from Black Mountain College had been traveling among the Lacandon people, researching backstrap loom weaving, when they'd been stopped by a group of armed militiamen. The militias strafed the river around their boat with bullets and motioned them ashore. "We were lucky," my friend said. The militias were likely less interested in robbing them (they only took his group's watches) than bored. After a few tense moments my friend and his companions clambered into their canoe and paddled away with all their strength, never looking back.

As it happens, that particular colleague was one of the first people I knew to receive a definitive HIV diagnosis at a time when testing was relatively new and treatment far in the future. It turned out that he was what would eventually be termed a "chronic nonprogressor" and survived for years. During that time, his friends succumbed, one by one, and so, too, did his partner, a Montessori school teacher, who, when he could no longer work, began spending his days at the *Voice* offices, on a flaking black Naugahyde sofa of unknown origin, pretending to read but mostly staring blankly at the office goings-on. He was a silent, doleful presence marking what remained of his time. No one asked why he was there, out of politeness or indifference, and then eventually, one day, he was not there anymore and without a word being spoken we all knew what that meant.

His partner, my colleague, stayed healthy and upbeat. The only obvious indication he had a sword dangling over his head was a sudden taste he developed for pricey Italian sweaters. It might be that he inherited some money at his boyfriend's death. In any event, and though he had never previously been a clotheshorse, he now swept into the offices dressed in expensive statement sweaters designed by Enrico Coveri, Gian Marco Venturi, Giorgio Armani. Labels still largely unknown at the time. His favorite was a Missoni cardigan with zigzag chevrons in varied shades of blue. Rudolf Nureyev, he said, owned a similar one, though Nureyev's surely didn't reek of mothballs that left my colleague in a haze of camphor that was its own kind of statement. He intended to outlast the moths.

It was the Missoni sweater he was wearing on the day he died, not of AIDS but from an ordinary heart attack that felled him on the platform of the R train at Union Square. He was fifty-one, and I remember thinking at the time of his as a long run and a good end, given what I had seen by then of wasted bodies, people robbed of mobility, continence, vision, most of them young men who fell to a litany of maladies like shigella, carcinoma, sarcoma, melanoma, glioma, glioblastoma, myeloma, and lymphoma, diseases so awful it seemed a far greater mercy to die fast.

o o o

HOME IN NEW YORK, Sylvia and I returned to what I think of as our people, each one a chapter or, let's say, an episode in an ongoing reality show. There was the sidewalk Santa with a shady Raymond Chandler backstory living in a Bowery

Timișoara, Romania, 1991
© Sylvia Plachy

flophouse where stewbums paid twenty-five cents to "sleep" on chairs while slumping against ropes slung between them. There were the Central Park zookeepers charged with tending the polar bear tank, a Beckettian assignment largely taken up to distract the animals from their captivity with tires and floats and other useless toys.

One week we found ourselves out in Coney Island visiting Lillie Santangelo, owner and proprietor of the World in Wax Musee. After fifty-six years in business, Lillie had decided to close up shop and sell off her collection of wax figures, many of which she'd commissioned herself and even painted using makeup brushes from Woolworth's. She used the brushes, as I wrote at the time, to lend "rougey vitality" to effigies of "moonlight stranglers, despots, and two-headed babies." Off to the auction block it would all go, the waxworks of Elvis Presley, Babe Ruth, Clark Gable, and Ruth Snyder, a murderess who got the electric chair for killing her jealous husband with a sash weight.

"They were my friends," Lillie said of figures sculpted by a talented Swedish drunk she put up for years in a room at the Half Moon Hotel. Every morning when she opened the Musee Lillie greeted the dummies by name. "Not just Jean Harlow, mind you," she said. "I'm just as polite to John Christie," she added, referring to a serial killer who romanced prostitutes in the East End of London, strangled them, then drained and sipped their blood.

"I had a letter from a fellow who knew John Christie," Lillie told me. "He said my figure of him looked better than the man himself."

There used to be a city filled with stories like Lillie Sant-angelo's; we don't live there anymore. Yet the tone I aim to set here is not elegiac. I'm as unsentimental about that time as Lillie was about her waxworks. When the time comes, you pack up and move on.

Sure, I miss the way that, in a predigital age, people entered one's frame of consciousness without the benefit of algorithms. The city gave me Adam Purple just as, for those of my parents' generation, it provided an avatar of the noble urban loner, in the form of Moondog, the blind "Viking of Sixth Avenue." For years, I'd seen Purple, a wizened character with long white hair and a trailing beard, a hippie hobbit dressed in head-to-toe lavender tie-dye, whizzing around town on his purple bicycle.

Suddenly I was moved to learn who he really was. I should not have been surprised to discover that he was no kook but a hard-nosed, passionate community activist, though that would have been the first guess of anyone sighting him pedaling furiously around town on his acid-trip wheels, hauling behind him a custom-built travois filled with horse manure. On daily rounds to Central Park and the livery stables on West Thirty-Eighth Street, Purple scavenged horse droppings he would use as compost for a garden that, together with his partner, Eve, he was constructing according to arcane cosmological precepts in an abandoned lot on the Lower East Side. They named it, logically enough, the Garden of Eden, and it was an illegally homesteaded community space occupying a blighted segment of Forsyth Street just behind Purple's walk-up apartment on Eldridge Street in an area where whole blocks of abandoned

Adam Purple, 1985
© Sylvia Plachy

tenements by then had been razed or allowed to burn or decay by the city and later sold to speculators who snapped up the land on the cheap. One outcome of all those stolid apartment houses being reduced to rubble was that there was an abundance of architectural salvage with which to construct the concentric paths and drylaid walls of Eden: limestone lintels, marble doorsteps, keystones and Belgian block, and all manner of building materials.

The city conveniently turned a blind eye to the Garden of Eden—which Adam and Eve cultivated entirely by hand, tools and machinery being considered "counterrevolutionary"—warehousing the land for a boomtown future that was not, after all, that far off. All those AIDS deaths were a great convenience to developers; each time death served its inexorable eviction notice to an artist, writer, poet, actor, dancer, or anyone else with the disease, another unit of housing returned to the open-market rent rolls.

By the time I met him, Purple's garden was already a goner, condemned by the city. Demolition crews were on the way. Whatever in the future supplanted this serene terrain with its fruit orchard and vegetable patches and wild grasses and pathways made from bricks rescued when the wrecking balls were done, what seemed certain was that it would be nothing like the prelapsarian garden conjured by a tie-dyed hippie and his common-law wife.

o o o

SURELY I WAS MISTAKEN. Of course there will always be determined idealists like those who nourish the writer I increasingly saw myself becoming, people like a Bronx grade-school teacher I met who organized Easter egg hunts for the children of parents addicted to crack or else guerrilla performance artists who roamed the streets of SoHo clad in trash-bag gowns and staged unauthorized "tours" of SoHo galleries or else pop-up protests of corrosive late-stage capitalism in the lobbies of banks, or even creatures like Richie Gallo, another unclassifiable whose spectacles "often incorporate long stretches of minimal movement juxtaposed with sudden physical outbursts," as one critic observed.

To the extent that anybody knew much about him, Gallo was "Lemon Boy," a reference to the absurdist happenings he mounted in public places, wearing, as often as not, little more than a fishnet bodysuit stretched over his taut, muscular body and doing strange things with fruit.

When we first met, Gallo had showed up on the steps of the Fifth Avenue main branch of the New York Public Library dressed in a leopard-print loincloth and matching mask. If an interview is a mostly one-sided dialogue with a sphinx, I conducted one with him. It was over in minutes and transacted mostly through mime. Simultaneously Gallo gave wordless directions to five veiled accomplices who unfolded and set up ironing boards in graduated rows between the library's stone lions, Patience and Fortitude.

With that task complete, the helpers proceeded to pace ritualistically between the ironing boards as Gallo crouched at the top landing and bowled lemons down the stairs. This routine was to be repeated in some form throughout the city, at Bloomingdale's near the cosmetics department; on the Fifth Avenue sidewalk outside Tiffany's; at the portal to the New

Richie Gallo, 1980
© Sylvia Plachy

York Stock Exchange. When I asked him to explain the meaning of his enigmatic antics he very briefly broke his silence: "Annoy the rich."

Gallo, unsurprisingly, vanished into obscurity, all but forgotten until resurrected years later by the internet. As grim as it will later become, the city remained for me then a place where encounters like that were, if not exactly routine, not rare. A further example is an artwork I fell upon that had been created by David Hammons, then an artist known to cognoscenti yet far from being the master he will later, universally, be deemed. Hammons was best known for his sly and fugitive artworks, art performances like a flash sale he staged one winter day outside the Cooper Union, laying out rows of individual snowballs, graduated in size, on a tarp and hawking them to passersby. Far less familiar is another of the curious gardens people cultivated in derelict spaces, this one a vacant lot shoehorned between commercial buildings on 125th Street off Fifth Avenue in Harlem.

What Hammons had done was to festoon the branches of scrawny weed trees with discarded bottles—mostly empties of Night Train, Thunderbird, and Wild Irish Rose or whatever fortified rotgut was being consumed thereabouts, bottles he collected on nightly rounds with a supermarket shopping cart. For an earlier artwork, Hammons had followed a similar routine, traveling to black barbershops to collect hair clippings that he afterward twined around metal bristles salvaged from a mechanical street-sweeper. He abandoned that project when he caught lice but for his practice continued to use refuse to make artworks that would later sell for millions and become the subject of museum retrospectives and adoring scholarly monographs.

A commonplace trope of critical writing about him holds that his work resonated with "pain, anger, and absurdity of being a black man in the United States," as *The New Yorker* put it. The artist I met was far too sophisticated and subtle to mire himself in the politics of identity. The youngest-born of ten children raised in near poverty near Springfield, Illinois, Hammons may have been interested in subverting the system; just as likely it delighted him to outwit it in the way of a prankster or griot, as he suggested when we spoke.

In the rare interviews he gives, Hammons can come off as a a droll Zen master, speaking in koans. He jokes about having traveled to Area 51 and found some socks there that he'd lost in the dryer. He talks about how it took him a lifetime to come around to jazz. He seldom fails to note how the true focus of his work is engagement with the world or about how his art materials, now and always, are whatever the streets provide.

For his "Bottle Garden," it was the empties found and washed and then wheeled to a lot that could only be reached by squeezing through a gap in the cyclone fencing. His inspiration for the "Bottle Garden," he told me, were those poetic yet practical gardens that can be spotted in broom-swept dirt yards across the rural South. In those places the purpose of the bottles is to trap malevolent spirits before they can cross the threshold and enter the household. The household here was Harlem and the brown or green or clear bottles slid over branches of scrubby ailanthus—stink tree—functioned as tal-

ismans, protective, but also commemorative of the local alco-
holics and what might easily be dismissed as disposable lives.

I thought then and think now of Hammons as a prophet
of the make-do, a canny philosopher whose improvised material was part of the point. In what society cast off he saw
the transcendent. In whatever was judged worthless—hair
clippings, rotgut empties, refuse, grease—he found materials for creating transformative emblems of what a curator
once called, a bit portentously for my taste, "the experience
of the outsider in the contemporary world." He accomplished
that, of course, yet with the mordant wit I associate with the
drag queens I'd known or those friends who rummaged for
treasures through thrift shops and curbside trash. I can easily
draw a line of kinship between Hammons and, say, Joseph
Cornell, another brilliant loner, in whose elegiac boxes—as
Octavio Paz wrote—"memory weaves, unweaves the echos."
Hammons, too, framed worlds made of his own devising
from junk like old wiffle balls, used medicine bottles, mar-
bles, newsprint cutouts, and dice.

Decades later, I found myself riding north along Third
Avenue from Chinatown one December afternoon in the
front seat of a ride share with just enough sky visible through
the windshield to remind me that out beyond the slot canyons
of midtown lay the rest of America. Though I love this view
at all hours, it is best on those late winter afternoons when
twilight slowly closes over the milky sky.

A couple in the back seat of the Toyota Camry sat scrolling
through their phone feeds, oblivious to anything outside their
screens. This now-defunct ride service had recently expanded

David Hammons in his "Bottle Garden," 125th Street, 1981
© Sylvia Plachy

to include the Bronx, and I was capitalizing on a bargain introductory fare to head up to Bedford Park Boulevard to see the old haunts. It was far from the first time I'd made the trek to the Bedford Court apartments, wandered the perimeter of a Catholic girls' school across the street before climbing the high stoop of the nondescript yellow-brick building where, in what was once Paula's and my first-floor apartment, signs now advertised the "Tiny Steps" daycare center. What did I hope to find here? I can only answer that with another question: What draws us back to the places where we were once young?

On one exploratory outing I'd walked all the way down from Bedford Park to the New York Botanical Garden, headed deep into the grounds to look for what I'd heard was a remnant of an old-growth forest. Sure enough, there it was: a fifty-acre parcel of primeval woods that must be what a virgin New World looked like to the first Europeans. That time I hoped to jostle something indeterminate in memory, some connection to my own past that hovered just out of reach. Instead, I got lost. This had the benefit of making me focus and for all I know was the unconscious point of the exercise. Though the past may not be dead or even past, this is not to suggest that you can ever go back there.

The car radio in the Via was tuned to some Sirius channel playing mainly old-school rap. Suddenly, though, the deejay cued up "Pump Up the Volume," that one-hit acid house wonder that is the Rosetta stone of lyrical sampling.

"I used to know a couple of those guys," I said to the driver.

"Which guys?"

"Eric B. and Rakim," I replied, assuming he'd recognize the names of the musicians whose earlier release "I Know

You Got Soul" was the source of so much in "Pump Up the Volume"—and, as far as I could guess, of half the popular music in any genre made ever since.

"I mean, not Rakim so much, more Eric B.," I added. "I met Rakim a bunch of times, but the person I was really close to was Eric B.'s mother-in-law."

And just like that it was as if we were back in 1987 and I was sitting in the living room of a cramped apartment in a third-floor walk-up ten minutes from the Brook Avenue stop on the 6. I can remember everything about the place: a brocaded polyester three-piece living room suite, two shiny armchairs that seemed to be covered in Teflon and bought on layaway, all the furniture crammed awkwardly into the center of the room for the simple although not immediately apparent reason that it was not safe to sit anywhere by a window during those South Bronx days.

Random gunfire was common. Over at the Highbridge Garden Homes a young rapper on the verge of stardom had just been shot to death by a gunman firing from an apartment window. Stray bullets meant for someone else might catch you or even ricochet. Death came out of nowhere. People had been killed while sleeping in their beds.

There was a bullet hole in the wall of the apartment, just above a glass étagère stacked with framed high-school photos and sports trophies. Someone happened to misfire a pistol inside the apartment. Someone else had surrounded the hole with metallic stick-on stars.

This was where Eric B.'s mother-in-law had lived for years and sometimes Eric B. himself and the woman's daughter, with whom he had a kid. Occasionally I visited this gentle but hard-nosed woman, a municipal worker who supported various members of her family, including a son who generally only turned up when he was coming down off drugs.

This was the era when crack and heroin were sold so brazenly in the open that South Bronx corners were busier than a Stop & Shop endcap during a Fritos blowout. When Social Services checks landed on the first of the month, the corner of Brook and St. Ann's Avenues looked like a ghoulish scene in an Otto Dix painting. Drug dealers suddenly appeared and crowds formed instantly, central casting junkies or crackheads with empty-eyed expressions, gripping bills in their sweaty fists. Where the characters depicted in German Expressionist paintings tended to look as though they reveled in depravity, these addicts were in considerable, very real pain. Without wanting to be melodramatic, it's not too much to say the hurt went deeper than withdrawal.

Sometimes when I went up there, I put my pad away. I stood back and watched the hectic scene from a distance. What it reminded me of was crystals clustering in the chamber of a kaleidoscope of jagged pieces forming geometric patterns through a viewfinder. Some mysterious physics seemed to govern those arrangements of fragments. Chaotic and formless, the mob immediately grew orderly when the dealer showed up. Two seconds after scoring the junkies scattered to shoot up in St. Mary's park, but the crackheads, who couldn't wait that long, immediately smoked up in the vestibules of nearby buildings.

Naturally the competition was so strong that they began marketing the goods in thirty-milligram glassines of heroin printed with their own individual dope stamps. The images

Brook Avenue, the South Bronx, 1988
© Sylvia Plachy

and emblems were mostly of skulls, knives, scorpions, spiders, donkeys, or anything that suggested the contents of the packets delivered an extra kick. The wittier dealers promoted their wares by tying them in to mainstream products, box-office hits, current events, or natural disasters. "Lethal Weapon" was popular for a while. So was "Hurricane" heroin right after Tropical Storm Gilbert was upgraded to a Category 5.

Crossing St. Ann's Avenue once on the way to my friend's apartment, I spotted a discarded dope packet printed with a funny brand name. Slipping it into the pocket of my jean jacket, I took it home to look at later on. For a while I kept it on my desk and then tossed it, forgetting all about it until suddenly I found myself explaining to this stranger at the wheel of my Via how the city felt to me in those days. I would guess-timate that the man was younger than me by a decade. Yet when I began to talk about the Bronx as I recalled it, about my social worker friend and her struggle to hold on to her family and the stability she labored all her life to create, he stopped me.

"What was the brand?" he asked.

"You're going to laugh," I told him.

"Try me."

"The brand was 'No Pain.'"

With that, and in an automatic way, I started riffling through a litany of reminiscences with this stranger, recalling first a deejay party some friends and I attended at the Bronx River Houses—where rap music got its start—and a later all-star show featuring the Sugar Hill Gang at the Harlem Armory. My pals and I got a bit stoned first for that one and then wished we hadn't when the music began and stopped almost at once, when someone yelled "gun" and everyone started stampeding for the doors.

"I'm not exactly saying I miss that New York," I said. "But I kind of do, in a way."

"I know, where's the flavor?" he said.

He mentioned then that things were still very rough in some parts of the Bronx, particularly where he lived up around Buhre Avenue. What was once a Jewish and then an Irish neighborhood was now mostly Albanian.

"They have their own law," he said. "Even NYPD leaves them alone."

"Check this out," he said then, bending his shirt collar to reveal a finger-wide keloid on his nape. It was an ugly, ropy scar where someone got sloppy closing the wound. He got cut, he said, when somebody jumped him. He didn't say how or why and I didn't ask him and we kept rolling through traffic until he turned west at the Sixty-Fifth Street transverse and stopped at a red light on Central Park West. Reaching down to roll up one pant leg, he showed me a crater in his right calf that looked like a war wound. "I really didn't feel the bullet," he said.

I'd heard that before, but only in the days when the weapons in use when people got shot were handguns. Unlike automatic weapons, pistol fire penetrates relatively neatly. As long as no organs are involved people often survive. That changed when assault weapons became easy to procure, since a bullet fired from an AR15, though it may go in cleanly, causes what forensic scientists coolly refer to as "radial acceleration, shear, stretch, and compression" as it exits.

"I didn't even realize what happened until I looked down

and my sneaker was full of blood," the driver said. Again I did not press for details because, if I have learned anything as a reporter, it is that when people have important things to tell you about themselves it is best to let them do it in their own time.

Once, long ago, my friend the novelist Gary Indiana griped about how New York had become a suburb of nothing. Like all New Yorkers (although Gary was born in New Hampshire, lived a lot in L.A. and Cuba, and now, for reasons of his own, also in Bucharest, his home base is a sixth-floor walk-up on East Eleventh Street with a tub in the kitchen and a toilet in a common hall), Gary meant by New York "the city" and by the city, of course, Manhattan.

I know how he feels. And yet I've disciplined myself not to get too attached to some fantasy of the boroughs, a gritty fantasia, a *CSI* set, Danger Disney. Still, I sensed that the driver and I had in common a shared slant on how much more alive the place felt when there were places you knew better than to be after hours, clubs that didn't cater to college freshmen with credit cards from their parents, when it was a proper underbelly and a real Tenderloin.

Impulsively, then, I asked if he'd ever been to Sally's Hideaway, a question with some risk in it since Sally's was a scuzzy dive bar on West Forty-Third Street frequented mostly by transvestite prostitutes and what you might call their admirers. It was also one of those spots where a surprising number of New Yorkers turned up at one time or another, one of those places that someone who knew somebody cool thought everyone ought to see once. At Sally's you also met the sex-show workers from Show World, a twenty-two-thousand-square-foot emporium (legally constituted as Show World Center) at the corner of Forty-Second Street and Eighth Avenue. They drank at Smith's bar, famous for its red neon sign facing Eighth and tabloid-notorious as the saloon where, in 1994, a police officer on his meal break drew out his .38-caliber service revolver and shot himself in the head. It surprised me to learn that sex-show performers mostly ordered club soda at bars until one of them explained that it was hard enough faking sex five times a day without being drunk.

"Well, I'm not saying I went to Sally's or I didn't go there," the driver said. "But you know, in this business, people are always looking for somewhere to drain a vein."

Back in the eighties I met a photographer trained by Walker Evans at Yale who after graduating came down from New Haven and rented a studio eight floors above the fluorescent peep show limbo of Show World to take portraits of sex workers. I met a lot of them through her and would never afterward look upon them as freaks.

From time to time my friend invited me to sit in on a portrait session and suggested that if the sex workers seemed willing, I could maybe write some stories about their lives.

I'm not especially proud to say how misguided my preconceptions were about these people. Some had grotesque or lurid backstories, but the majority were the same working people you'd stand behind on a checkout line. One was a Barnard graduate powering through a doctoral thesis on Jacques Lacan, another a young Latina singer with a lisp and an act involving a pet Burmese python that she fed live mice. One was a dwarf (he hated "little person") with a penis the length of a kickstand. If anything was surprising about these people who stripped every day for strangers and simulated various sex acts it was how shy they were in front of a lens.

"Why were you asking about Sally's?" the driver said.

I skipped the story about the Forty-Second Street studio and instead launched into a tale about an artist friend and her gay husband who once took me to Sally's and then, afloat on lines of some very good coke, onward uptown to Andre's in Harlem.

Andre's is gone now, of course. There is a nine-screen Magic Johnson multiplex where it once stood. The theater anchors the Harlem USA mall, an ugly glass box that cost a lot of public money to build and that opened on the cusp of the millennium with a ribbon-cutting ceremony and a passel of politicians trying to get in on the black vote. To read newspaper accounts of the time you might have thought that razing a collection of century-old buildings, mom-and-pop shops, and other local institutions and supplanting them with a generic mall was an act of the greatest civic munificence. The city's most important paper covered the event as though one of the more historically layered neighborhoods had been a cultural desert until developers finally provided it with a Disney store, an HMV, and an Old Navy outlet.

Sometimes now I ride a bus up from my apartment to Harlem to catch an Imax film at the Magic Johnson. When I do, my mind inevitably strays to that night at Andre's, an old-time barn of a gay bar that replaced another establishment called the Silver Rail. These thriving landmarks had, successively, been in operation for the better part of a half century, serving generations of gay Harlemites. It was at Andre's that my artist friend and her gay husband and the sex-show worker with the Lacan dissertation fell in that long-ago night with a formidable drag queen called Grace—just Grace.

We were introduced by Smitty, the bartender, though "introduced" may be misstating things, since my artist pal was the sort of person most people felt they had known forever within two minutes of making her acquaintance. Understandably much of what remains is a blur. But I recall with perfect clarity Grace's linebacker shoulders, her ice-blue brocade cocktail dress, the silver-tipped mid-calf mink she wore and how it set off the unusual steel gray of her updo wig.

It was Grace who suggested we beat it out of Andre's and she who led us around the corner through the bitter cold into another bar on the north side of 125th Street. Wedged into the ground floor of a brownstone, paces from the Apollo Theater marquee, was a shoebox-size room with a long bar rail and a clientele very different from Andre's. At Jay's the patrons were of two types, either B-boy hustlers in do-rags and thin leather jackets or johns with a taste for rough trade and former jailbirds.

What I cannot recall anymore is how Grace came to introduce us to the stranger sitting on one of Jay's barstools. Anomalous in the setting, she was nursing a Bacardi and Coke and wore a honey-blond bouffant, a crepe dress with a plunging neckline, and a deeply weary expression.

This was Dorian Corey. At the time I am writing about, in the early 1980s, Jennie Livingston's documentary *Paris Is*

Burning was still in production and had not yet introduced to the wider world its revelations about a little-known ballroom scene with its infinitely sophisticated cultural critiques and complex social structures—various "houses" named for European fashion designers were run by dictatorial if often loving "mothers" who parented wayward queer and trans children cast out of their birth households and just as frequently inducted them into crime syndicates specializing in shoplifting, identity theft, and credit card fraud.

Madonna's hit song and video "Vogue" was off in the future. So was *RuPaul's Drag Race* and the improbable idea of drag becoming a lucrative career track. Academic gender studies, too, were in their infancy then, and so voguing balls remained much as they'd been when Langston Hughes described them as "the strangest and gaudiest of all Harlem spectacles." That is to say the balls were wondrous, and among the reasons was that they were still run by personages—foremothers of renegade queerness— such as Dorian Corey.

"Do you remember someone called Dorian Corey?" I asked the Via driver. "Drag queen, died in the early nineties."

"Maybe," he said.

"Sure, you do," I replied. "They found a mummy in her apartment after she died."

"Oh, yeah," he said. "Didn't I read that in the *Post*?"

"*New York* magazine did a big story afterward," I said. The headline on that piece was "The Drag Queen Had a Mummy in Her Closet."

And it was true. She did.

"Yeah, right," the driver said with a laugh.

"If you can believe it I used to play Scrabble with her in that same apartment."

How the body of a small-time criminal named Robert "Bobby" Worley ended up in that closet on West 140th Street and St. Nicholas Avenue, in a once-staid part of town that later degenerated into a crack-infested and perilous no-man's-land, is a mystery that has never been solved. Bound in duct tape, swaddled in Naugahyde, and stuffed into a garment bag, Worley's body had been packed into a piece of oversized luggage and tucked away among Dorian's feather boas, a bullet through its head and some pop-tops from beer cans inadvertently stuck to the sticky-tape shroud. No one could ever determine how long the mummified corpse had been there, though forensic experts later estimated Worley had been dead about twenty years based on the last time that type of pop-top was in manufacture.

Bobby Worley, with all due respect, doesn't matter to me now. What does is that introduction to Dorian, which, through an unlikely sequence of otherwise meaningless events, led to me visiting her on occasion at that Harlem apartment, losing at Scrabble while gaining an education in class and gender and the bitterly negotiated strategies of survival in a world that had effectively condemned this superior being to live in a storm drain. Strangely I recall nothing unusual about the atmosphere of the apartment; rather, it was no more odd than plenty of places I had been. I do recall that it was always redolent of an incense, a type sold by Muslim vendors on subway platforms. Later, I learned that the brand was called "Night Queen."

All this took place before I had ever been to a vogue ball. All this took place before I had attended gatherings like Pepper LaBeija's "The Night All the Stars Came Back Out" extravaganza, with categories that included a variety of metaconcepts related to the notion of "realness."

Realness would eventually pass into mainstream parlance, as would other honed enhancements on performative human artifice. At ballroom events like "Costume Extraordinaire," there were competitive categories like "Night Stalker Part II, 43rd Street and 8th Avenue vs. 14th Street & 9th Avenue." The point was that masculine-leaning people masqueraded as female-identified sex workers in streetwalker drag calibrated to appeal to denizens of competing strolls. Trans hookers in Times Square had one look. Girls in the Meatpacking District were less "classy," which meant they often went around with their miniskirts pulled up to expose male genitals. For a while I collected flyers from these balls—notable for clumsy graphics and instructions scripted like parodies of semiotics texts—but eventually they got lost.

I did hold on to one for a ball staged by the House of Ultra Omni at the Prince George Ballroom, a flyer with guidelines for "walking" in categories like "Butch Queen Realness." "We are not looking for a butch queen that looks like a real man," it read. "We want a real man. We're looking for someone who has never walked a ball before but most importantly has never had sex with another man . . . yet! Not realness but true reality."

Dorian Corey was born Frederick Legg in Buffalo, New York, in 1937. Frederick Legg, in trans parlance, was Dorian's deadname.

When she killed off the identity assigned her at birth and

replaced it with that of an elegant, if blowsy, female enter-
tainer in the Josephine Baker mold is unclear. But as Dorian
Corey she was already touring in a snake dance act in the
Pearl Box Revue by the 1960s. Soon afterward she established
the House of Corey and began accumulating grand prizes at
voguing balls at such a rate that she soon transcended elite
legendary status and was apotheosized in the ballroom world
as an "Icon." Yet Dorian's was not parodic realness; she lived
as a woman, what she called "true reality."

There is a scene in *Paris Is Burning* that is perhaps its
most famous. In it Dorian sits at a dressing table in front of
a makeup mirror "beating her face." Her hair is pulled taut
under a banded taupe wig base. Tendrils from a half-smoked
Winston twist through the frame.

By now the Via driver had traversed the Grand Concourse
and reached Bedford Park Boulevard. I can remember feeling sympathy for the guy, thinking about how many random
fragments he must have heard from the lives of strangers. At
least in my line of work we are paid to listen, if not always to
make sense of what people choose to tell us and what they
hold back. With a few blocks left and with that thought in
mind I hazarded a few questions: What really happened, how
had he gotten stabbed and shot; also, what had brought him to
a joint like Sally's Hideaway in the first place?

"Long story," he said.

"I know," I replied. "Is there a short version?"

"I used to be another person," the driver told me. "Got
myself involved in things I shouldn't have and let life run me.
That was a different time and, you know, a different city: I
was another person."

I understood that he was saying it was none of my concern and that ten seconds after I got out he would pick up the next fare—with any luck someone heading back to Manhattan—and forget me. I, on the other hand, would replay our conversation, review it again in a variety of lights as I attempted to get hold of how we, so many of us, perhaps everyone, come to cycle through many lives in the course of a single existence.

The mercury seemed to have plummeted in the time it took us to reach the Bronx. I changed my mind abruptly about revisiting the old haunts, which now filled me with an unaccountable sense of dread, a cluster of unrelated images, all related to the cold, rising up in memory: bitter wind cutting through my flimsy bomber jacket as Paula and I trudged home at dawn from the Tenth Floor; snow numbing my feet in that driveway off Vineyard Road; that paralyzing sense of grief that threatens to overtake you when a loved one dies, a frozenness that nothing can convince you will ever thaw.

Toward the conclusion of *Paris Is Burning,* Dorian Corey does a marvelous thing. The theatrical world-weariness she affected for the camera seems to vanish and you realize it was not an act. Dorian had barely crossed into her fifth decade when the documentary was being made and would die of AIDS not many years after its release. In her relatively short span, she experienced more than her share of tragedy, including the obvious and fundamental one of knowing deep in her bones how many people in the world fervently contested her right, as a black, gay trans woman, to exist.

But Dorian had no time for lamentation; it wasn't her style. In the film's final setup, she lowers and, all but imperceptibly, flutters the lids of eyes fringed with a double row of false lashes. Her dressing gown has fallen open; you can see breast implants beginning to sag with age.

When I replay the scene in my memory it summons for me the heady incense that permeated Dorian's overheated apartment, the sound of the M3 bus grinding down St. Nicholas Avenue outside, and her droll habit of playing off those who suffered from the widely distributed delusion that human will has much of anything to do with fate.

"I always had hopes of being a big star," Dorian says to the middle distance, her gaze directed somewhere beyond the lens of the camera.

"As you get older, you aim a little lower," she adds. "Everybody wants to leave some impression, some mark upon the world; now I think you've left a mark upon the world if you just get through it and a few people remember your name. You don't have to bend the whole world. Pay your dues and enjoy it. If you shoot an arrow and it goes real high—hooray for you."

o o o

IT WILL BE OBVIOUS by now to a reader that I did not know my father. The man that, for a long time, I imagined I understood—fantasist, fabulist, absent husband and father, nutjob entrepreneur with, unfortunately, no head for business—remained in most basic ways a mystery to me until his abrupt death at ninety-two. Because my dad had made no more provisions for his old age than for practical matters at any other stage of his life, I used to joke with my brother, Glenn, that he had better hope, when his time was up, that the hammer came down quickly. This, in fact, did occur.

In sturdy health, apart from some manageable hypertension, he had signed up for one of the hip replacements that are considered medically routine even among nonagenarians. The surgery was a success, as expected; four days after going under the knife he transferred to a step-down unit to undergo physical therapy before his release. He was unhappy with the new room; the nurses annoyed him. They were less attentive than those on the surgical floor, which I took to mean they didn't laugh at his jokes.

He told me this on the phone the night after his transfer. He was in Baltimore and I was in San Francisco, where I had gone to escape the pandemic sirens wailing night and day through my neighborhood in Manhattan. My dad noted on the phone that the new hip was designed to last at least another thirty years. He was not exactly kidding when he added that he'd already signed up for the next replacement. He also said he was craving a strawberry margarita when he got out, which struck me as odd since all his life his drink had been a manhattan. Then I recalled my brother mentioning that Dad could only drink clear spirits these days. Brown liquor brought out the bitterness and anger he'd spent years concealing. "One scotch," Glenn said, "and he starts sounding like some Fox News crazy."

When my cell phone rang at five the next morning I was, as it happened, a little hungover myself. It was Glenn on the line. "Dad died," he said, and I absorbed the bluntness of the news as if someone had slugged me.

Sometime early that morning, an embolism traveling from my father's leg to his lung blocked blood flow to his heart and that was it. A nurse looked in at seven and found him sleeping. When she checked again a half hour later he was dead. "He was alive until he wasn't," a friend would later remark, and I found the thought consoling. Just like that, it was done.

I showered and pulled on a hoodie, leaving the house where I was staying and heading by instinct into the nearby Presidio on foot. It was too early on the East Coast to call anyone I knew and so I took to the trails in that bone-chilling San Francisco summer cold, oblivious to the dense fog that comes in off the ocean to blot out the sky and snag in the branches of the Monterey cypress or even the usual posted alerts, always to be taken seriously, about this being the season when the park's coyotes were whelping.

A foghorn sounded to mark the tide surge through the Golden Gate off of Fort Point, the bridge itself invisible, as was the bay and even the trail two feet in front of me. Earlier in that same summer, before my dad died, I finally got around to putting questions to him I should have asked long ago. They were about my grandfather's death in a train crash many decades earlier. Although this event reverberated in subterranean ways through all our lives, I realized I knew little about this man who existed as a kind of phantom, formless, a thought broken off midsentence.

Throughout childhood I was aware that something terrible had happened long ago though I never knew its details. What little I knew about the event was half-remembered from a newspaper clipping happened upon once in my aunt's attic. What I thought I recalled from overheard conversation was that my grandfather had been a gifted natural athlete, a sailor and avid fisherman. Lake, river, or ocean; hook-and-line, fly-fishing, or surf-casting—it was all the same to him.

Am I dreaming that I recalled once hearing how, on the day he died, the bluefish were running and that he had a plan to drive out to Jones Beach Island and catch some? How can I know that the fishing party was meant to consist of my dad and his own father and a colleague from *The Bronx Home News,* where Victor C. Trebay ran the ad department? Among the pictures that survived the fire is one of him and my father standing atop a rock ledge in the woods, in shade, an older man and a child somewhere in Vermont.

Both are peering at something in the distance—maybe a waterfall, to judge by the setting. Who would have taken the photograph, though? And who was this remote if benevolent-looking man in the bucket hat?

Where, too, had these memories come from, these stories I patched together from fragments that could just as easily have been imagined as true? Had I invented the notion that my dad survived that day because he stayed back with a sore throat?

Am I alive to write this because he lazily pulled the covers over his head and unknowingly condemned someone else to die in his place?

A few years back I retraced the route they took that morning or, rather, that I believed they had. Based on what few shreds of information I possessed, I drove from my apartment in Manhattan to East 193rd Street in the Bronx and then began again as if that were my starting point, cutting through the darkness along a route that took me to the the old Whitestone Bridge and from there across the East River, where the bridge road merges with the Cross Island Parkway. I followed that east to an exit for Route 25A, then down a shady semi-rural two-lane that now passes for countless miles through the monotonous suburbs that only came into existence after the Second World War.

Before then, a surprising amount of Long Island remained farmland, a fact that changed after the government created the GI Bill to give returning vets a chance to set themselves up again in civilian lives. Much of the South Shore then was still a primordial glacial flatland; the Long Island Expressway wouldn't be extended into Nassau County for another decade after 1947, and the land I was driving through, the original Hempstead Plains, must still have resembled Fitzgerald's "great green breast" of the New World.

In a few miles the road joins the Meadowbrook Parkway, where the landscape flattens and the hilly North Shore woods give way to scattered thickets of pitch pine and bearberry scrub. Here begin the shimmering salt marshes fringing the Great South Bay, small scattered hummocks with houses perched on them and low bridges connecting the mainland with its sheltering barrier islands. Here, where the boundaries blur between sky and land, you can already sense the lambent light that artists seem to love.

As I pointed the rental car toward Babylon, I followed a route I'd determined must be the one my grandfather and his companions took that summer morning, traveling south over a grade crossing in Babylon that straddles the tracks of the Long Island Rail Road. In future years, automated warning

whistles would be installed to sound when advancing loco-
motives were a quarter mile out. In future years, computer-
ized level-crossing predictors would trigger flashers and bring
down cantilevered crossbucks to block traffic until a train had
safely gone by.

In 1947, however, approaching trains were flagged at cross-
ings, if at all, with manually operated barricades called "wig-
wags." This little detail would have no real significance were
it not that my entire personal narrative turned on a series of
entirely arbitrary elements, among them the random fact that,
as late as 1947, Long Island was very lightly populated; that
less than a quarter of Americans owned a car; that the railroad industry then was widely privatized and only subject to
the most limited government regulations. There is something
else. Caution signals at tracks intersecting country roads were
all but nonexistent.

I drifted a bit mentally on this predawn drive, trying to
summon a picture of the day my grandfather died, fantasiz-
ing about the three men in the car sharing a thermos of coffee,
talking quietly about their jobs and how good it would feel to
finally pull on their waders and cast lines into the surf zone
known as "the skinny." It was easy enough to conjure the hypnotic quiet of an empty night road because I was on one now.
But when I caught myself picturing a hazy blue dawn and a
car stalling in dense ground fog on a railroad crossing somewhere out near Babylon, that line of thinking came up short. I
was in the realm of speculation.

I returned in my thoughts to a famous 1946 crash I'd once
researched, a catastrophe dating from a time when railroad
companies were responsible for setting their own speed lim-

its. Heading west from Union Station in Chicago, a passenger train called the Advance Flyer slowed on the tracks just long enough to be rammed from behind at speed by another train, the Exposition Flyer. Forty-five people died in the crash, and only after the disaster did the Interstate Commerce Commission issue an order restricting the speed of passenger trains lacking automated control systems to seventy-nine miles per hour. That order was dated 1947 but would not be implemented for another four years. According to eyewitness estimates, the Exposition Flyer had been traveling at ninety miles an hour at the time of the crash. I thought as I drove about what a six-thousand-ton train moving at that speed might do to a stationary object.

As it turned out, very little of what I thought I knew about this long-ago event happened as I imagined. Retracing my grandfather's route was more of an act of imagination than fact-finding on my part since, I would come to know, Victor C. Trebay died not at dawn but at 11:38 in the morning, not in fog but in a light rain with otherwise clear visibility, not on his way to Jones Beach Island but rather sixty-three miles northeast of there at a spot where the two-lane Sag Harbor Turnpike intersects a different set of railroad tracks, a road I have driven on a thousand times.

He was riding that day in the back seat of a car whose driver was twenty-four-year-old George Meyer. Also with Meyer was Conrad Sheer, age fifty-seven. I have no idea who these men were and only know their names because I stumbled one day upon a pile of dated newspapers while rummaging through the aisles of an East Hampton thrift shop. Overpriced as they were at five dollars apiece, I bought them anyway on impulse and brought them home, and there it immediately was: page one, top right of the *East Hampton Star,* May 22, 1947, nestled amid news items of the sort you'd expect to find in a regional weekly serving an oceanside farming community that, for three months a year, became a resort for America's wealthiest people. During that week, I learned, General Norman T. Kirk, the surgeon general of the United States, and Mrs. Kirk took up residence at their new home in Montauk, where the newly retired general hoped "to do a great deal of fishing"; Bohack's supermarket broke ground for a planned new store at the corner of Fithian Lane and Main Street; Whitsunday services were scheduled for 10:45 at Saint Luke's Episcopal Church in East Hampton; votes were tallied for both Miss Jean Filer and Miss Lillian Stella, local nominees for queen of the annual Long Island Potato Festival; and this also happened: "3 Killed at Bridgehampton Crossing."

My own father was dead by the time I made this discovery. So, too, were his sisters and anyone else I might name from his generation and so, as I read the yellowed regional weekly, I felt not only sadness but great aloneness. There it all was, scarcely two hundred words pertaining to three men who "lost their lives last Sunday when their automobile was in collision with an eastbound Long Island Rail Road passenger train." Something about the use of the past continuous tense and its indirection caught me off guard. It was that assertion that by some unknown confluence of circumstances the car carrying my grandfather had been "in collision" with a speeding train. Unattributed sources were quoted as having said that "the three men arrived in this vicinity about 1 a.m. Sunday, evidently to go fishing." The car must have been obliterated, its passengers and contents scattered all over the track, and yet, by the terms of this bland account, it was the auto that somehow ran into a train, only to be "carried 80 feet," before it gently "slid down an embankment."

Passenger George Meyer died instantly. Conrad Sheer died in an ambulance on the way to Southampton Hospital. Still alive somehow when he was taken from the scene, Victor C. Trebay survived another few hours. If, by the logic of an overused formulation, we tell ourselves stories in order to live, what am I to make of a story like this? "The warning bell was in operation," the *East Hampton Star* of May 22, 1947, reported about the train crash that killed my grandfather, while failing to note the one element you'd want to know: Did it ring?

Once, when I was around seven, my dad brought me to visit my widowed grandmother at her Bronx apartment. What I remember best from that day is a bunch of cork-handled bamboo fishing rods bundled in a corner of the hall closet, alongside some rubber waders hung by their suspenders. Tucked on a shelf behind my grandmother's Persian lamb coat was a tackle box that I snuck out of the closet while the adults were chatting. Sitting on a white hobnail bedspread in a guest bedroom I examined its contents: hooks, trout flies, lures tied with bright thread, hackle feathers, shreds of fur. Some of the flies were so old and fragile that they threatened to fall to dust at the touch. Tucked at the bottom of the box was a leather case with a snap lid; inside it was a costly Pflueger Baitcast reel, from which I infer that my grandfather liked quality things, solid equipment, as I also do.

On the phone in the year before my father died, I asked him what he recalled of his dad. Abruptly he changed the subject. Changing tack, I asked instead about a funeral. Had there been one? I know there was a burial because I've sometimes visited the grave site in Port Washington.

Once again he deflected my question to speak instead about a relative I knew very little. "He was very decent to me" after the accident, my father said of this man.

How?

"He put his arm around me and said that he would be there for me as a kind of quasi-adult person if needed."

"Did he really use those words?" I asked. "'A kind of quasi-adult person'?"

"Something like that," my father said, and the possibility struck me that no one had ever revealed to him the truth about the accident, told him the true story of the automobile that ran into a train and the train that sent it into a ditch to shatter in an instant the futures of three men on a simple fishing trip. Maybe, also, his reluctance to participate in any meaningful way in my life was part of that inheritance; he passed along to me what little he had.

"Could he have meant 'like a father'?" I asked my dad.

"Yes, like a father," he said.

o o o

THE PLACE WHERE I am writing this is a log cabin in rural Virginia. The cabin is one in a cluster of similar structures built on the property of a Tidewater plantation. On this land in 1807 the most revered of Confederate generals was born. This man spent no more than his first three years here, yet the house has always been more intimately associated with him than with his illustrious forbears who included among them two signers of the Declaration of Independence. These days this man's name is spoken, if at all, in whispers. Artifacts from his life are stored here. A curator here once showed me the soldier's famous hat. There are log cabins on this property erected in the 1930s as guesthouses soon after the disintegrating brick manor house was saved from ruin, along with its dairy, farmhouses, spring house, a gristmill, an octagonal brick pavilion, a stone mausoleum, several fieldstone dependencies that are remnants of housing for enslaved people, as well as gardens planted with magnolia and parterres of bosomy *Buxus sempervirens* Suffruticosa.

I am here because a friend did me a kind deed. This friend is a director of a preservationist group dedicated to maintaining this historic house and its lands. When, in December of 2011, Dana's husband called me at my office one morning to say that she had died suddenly in the night, I became so delirious that I walked off my job and across Forty-Second Street, boarded a Circle Line ferry barely knowing I had done so, and rode in a trance for countless circuits of Manhattan, so many that I lost track of how often we had passed the Statue of Liberty and her damnable torch.

And when afterward my friend called to offer me a quiet place to go, she was too fastidious to mention grieving; I have sometimes observed that those who know you best tend to provide what you most need when you cannot name it. In the years since my sister's death I have returned here, with some regularity, to write. This is not because the place is convenient; it is a backwater in a literal sense.

The nearest international airport is seventy miles distant

and the closest town a six-mile drive by way of the serpentine route I prefer along Wild Sally Road. Before industrial agribusiness colonized the area and seeded fields with genetically modified soy, the local town was a thriving hub for family farming, logging, fishing, and crabbing. It is a drowsy spot now, hardly more than an elbow on a two-lane with a speed trap set to twenty miles per hour. The permanent population is under four hundred and to service it there is a convenience store, a Dollar Tree, and a laundromat patronized mainly by seasonal migrant pickers. There are two restaurants. One serves fried oysters, catfish platters, and budget spaghetti dinners on plates the size of a hubcap. I have never felt hungry enough to eat at the other, a place called "Yesterday's."

The preserve is reached by a scenic route called History Land Highway. In a banner year, this historic house and its grounds may see thirty thousand visitors. There have not been many banner years since I began visiting my friend's cabin. On occasion, after the last paying guest has driven off and the entrance gate swings shut, the only ones left on the plantation are some maintenance personnel and myself. Two feet outside a wan circle of porch light the night is inky and impenetrable. Since the cabin door lacks a latch, I'll occasionally light a fire to cut the silence.

At the foot of the cabin path stands a small fieldstone monument covered with lichen. Affixed to it is a weathered bronze memorial marker installed in the 1930s. The plaque commemorates—in raised letters and in the benighted language of an earlier era—this as the place "where are buried those Negroes who served so faithfully on this plantation."

Lately visitors have begun to return here in increasing numbers.

Many view the high cliffs at the end of the farm road, cliffs that stretch for miles upriver along the Potomac and that are remnants of an ancient seabed. So rich in fossils, these palisades are like a kind of geological nougat. When storms roll in off the Chesapeake Bay, debris sloughs from the cliffs and bone prospectors suddenly turn up with dig sticks and buckets, searching for vestiges of creatures that were alive twenty million years back.

Back in seventh grade, I had a geeky girlfriend who won a ribbon for a science project based on her family trips to a place like this, where they hunted for prehistoric shark teeth.

No matter how hard I try, I never find anything special on the beach when I go looking. Finally, frustrated, I bought a megalodon tooth from a local dealer. The fossil broker insisted I remove my shoes at the door of his house, notable for being entirely covered in white carpeting, and charged me thirty dollars. It seemed like a lot at the time, though it turned out to be a bargain. The tooth is half the size of my palm, and sometimes I hold it and think about how, in the Renaissance, fossilized relics like this were thought to be the petrified tongues of dragons or else how humanly impossible it is to fathom the abstraction of twenty million years.

For quite a long time it seemed nobody bothered much about the memorial boulder; scrawny oak saplings sprouted around it and the stone became overgrown with poisonous vines. Eventually, though, the board members confronted some equally poisonous facts about our shared American history, the ones so many of us ignored for too long or content-edly smothered in myth. They did this as a matter of decency as well as for the survival of this place they cherished and also because the tides of history, once reversed, cannot be held back. And now a tidy paved path of crushed oyster shells leads to the boulder, and strangers with no particular interest in magnifi-cent eighteenth-century manors come with some frequency to leave offerings of cowrie and oyster shells, glass beads, dried flowers, coins, tobacco, or bourbon. Now a website features a timeline extending backward through history to the indig-enous peoples and to that moment in the early eighteenth cen-tury when sixty enslaved Africans were first imported here as cargo from the Senegambia region, the Gold Coast, or the Gulf of Guinea (an unspecified number were also brought from Saint Helena Island, which is 1,200 nautical miles from the West African coast and 6,000 from Virginia).

Most of these humans were consigned to the original plan-tation builder for future sale as human chattel; a number he retained for himself. These people and their descendants went on to construct the great house and its dependencies; fire the bricks for the project from clay dug on the property; cut and mill enough virgin timber from the surrounding old-growth forests to lay the twenty-foot-long poplar floorboards that are one of the glories of a central great room. These people, who performed any and every other job necessary to the building of an important Tidewater estate and the wealth that flowed from it, were the "Negroes who served so faithfully on this plantation." Certain of their given names were recorded in documents kept by the plantation overseer and these, we are told, allow us to "interpret their lives more vividly." Most, of course, died anonymous and unrecorded. The "names and details" of their lives, according to the website, have been "lost in history."

I sometimes contemplate this phrase on my walks here, its case-closed finality and bland resolution into unknowing. I also think about a question I might have asked myself all along on my walks past the monument, sixty steps from the stone to the cabin door. Isn't it likely that all around us in our lives, not only in the South, lie old bones and unmarked burial places? I have observed them close at hand at the killing fields of Cambodia and seen them at Potter's Field on Hart Island and also along Murder Mile in Iraq. I have felt, at certain times, that even Manhattan—perhaps especially Manhattan—is densely populated with the disturbed spirits of friends who died young, mainly although not exclusively of AIDS. I encounter their ghosts and sense their presence, like ghosts in the Bardo, still attempting to find their way home, unwilling to admit they are dead.

For eight straight days during my first summer in Virginia, a large digital thermometer outside a local bank never once dropped below a hundred degrees during daylight hours. Without real air-conditioning in the cabin there was just one way to get cool, and that was to cruise around in my rental car. I thought a lot on those drives about my younger sister, Dana, and how only a year before her death she'd received reports indicating she had "beaten" her cancer. The decisive phrase used by the doctors at the Mayo Clinic was NED: no evidence of disease. Six months earlier her prognosis had been so hopeless it reminded me of a story I'd read about a woman who asked her doctors how long she had before her cancer killed her. The doctor replied: How long is a piece of string?

The experimental treatment Dana undertook at Mayo was not supposed to have worked; in fact, her application for the novel protocol was rejected at first because the case was too risky. An unsuccessful outcome would bring down the hospital's survival rate. Because Dana had already been treated before for cancer, she approached methodically what amounted to a death sentence.

She was not warrior-like about it because she saw combat metaphors for what they are: something to reassure the healthy. Statistical outcomes, she knew, are exactly the same for so-called fighters as for those who turn their faces to the wall. Dana was aware of all this when she first got her diagnosis and was also someone willing to take on risky odds.

"Percentages are percentages," she said. "They say there's a five percent chance [of survival]," she told me. "Who says I'm not in that five percent?"

On my drives along History Land Highway I thought about how it had never been in Dana's nature to complain. During our mother's Depression-era stay in the orphanage she suffered from agonizing earaches. Knowing there was no one to console her, she willed herself not to cry. Dana, too, had terrible earaches as a child, and she also willed herself into a stillness so absolute that we siblings sometimes felt we ought to check her breathing. That stoicism of hers haunts me sometimes, when I think back to the two of us as kids once huddling alone in a freezing Hillman Minx waiting for our dad to return from a hospital emergency room with Laura, who had cracked her skull, or how matter-of-fact she was in discussing the cancer that cost her a pregnancy, her ovaries, and both breasts when she was thirty-five. On my drives I rehearse the circumstances of her death, how she'd left their shared bedroom in her house outside Seattle and lain on the living room floor because she felt so sick she'd been afraid to cry out and wake her husband. So went the story he told me.

It was not the cancer that killed my sister. An abdominal infection overrode an immune system that, decimated by chemotherapy and radiation, spiraled into septic shock. When Dana's husband called with the news, he wept on the phone and said that if only Dana had roused him they might have made it to the emergency room. She let him sleep and went to the living room instead to die on the floor.

Sometimes on those drives along History Land Highway, I wondered what Dana would make of a piece of family history I came upon, a revelation I might never have had were she to have lived. Occasionally she and I discussed genealogy and how certain families reverentially recorded lineages in the back of inherited Bibles while we had little more than some fabricated nonsense sketched out in Hawaiian Surf sales brochures. Because it was tantalizingly easy to do, I got sucked into buying an online subscription to an ancestry site, the one run by the Church of Jesus Christ of Latter-day Saints.

Unsure at first which path to take on the site, I randomly typed the name of my maternal grandfather. Orson Dallas Foster seemed unusual enough that it could lead to something. And it did. Links quickly appeared, names branching to other names. From a maternal grandmother named Anna Dallas I was led to Asbury Dallas and his wife, Eliza Mickel, and then back in time to James Alexander Peyton Dallas and Sarah Hardesty, each link appearing as a sprightly green leaf at the top right corner of a box containing a generic male or female silhouette. Birth and death dates where known were provided, as well as locations. Clicking on one link after another I quickly transited three centuries that encompassed persons previously unknown to me: Alexander Dallas and Wife; Alexander Craven Dallas and Agnes Pollok; Violet Peyton, born in the Virginia Colony around 1656; and Francis Hardisty Hardesty, a soldier in the American Revolution.

By now, too, as I would later learn from further hints and tips that the website provided at additional cost, I had traced the roots of one branch of my family to an area between the Potomac and the Rappahannock Rivers not twenty miles north of the navy's Experimental Test Range at Pumpkin Neck. That is, a half hour's drive from where I was sitting.

Before coming here I had never given a moment's thought to Virginia, let alone to this obscure corner of the state, and this coincidence jolted me much as the occasional upriver blast from the Dahlgren site did. Suddenly the cabin might shudder and the ground literally shift beneath me. I felt an urge to share my findings with someone; instinctively my hand reached for the phone to dial Dana.

Pinned above the desk at the cabin was a note from a writer friend for whom loss was the main subject of her late literary life. When Dana died, this friend emailed her condolences and—given how much of her late work concerned the intractable grief that lodged in her core following the death of her husband and then her daughter—what she wrote was surpris-

Dana Trebay, 1974

ing. "In the end our siblings may be our truest relationships" were her words.

◦ ◦ ◦

HER HAIR WAS the first thing I noticed about the woman angling through the door of a restaurant in Dayton, even before catching sight of her face. The blond must come from a bottle by now, but the hair, falling past her shoulders, was as thick and lustrous as ever. It was cut in a style too young for a woman her age—she was in her sixties by now—and disarming considering that when I last saw her we were both in our early twenties. Her years on the run have taken a toll, but she's retained her good looks: the sharp cheekbones; the high-bridged nose, broken at one point; the taut economical mouth.

A waitress brought us to an exposed corner table—not what I'd hoped for in the way of privacy—and we paused for a light, tentative hug before sitting. The trench coat she had on over her wrap dress was too light for the weather and she looked very thin; hugging her, I could feel the sharp contours of her shoulder blades through the cloth.

Flying into Dayton, I gazed down on a gray-green patchwork of fallow winter fields spreading out in all directions and cut through by occasional ribbons of interstate. I mentioned to my sister how I had never given much thought to the scale of the city where she lived, had not realized how rural the surrounding area was. I mentioned a brochure I found in my hotel room that made note of a local Air Force base with a population that fluctuated around thirty thousand, and added that I would never have guessed that from the empty highways I drove on, which looked as though there had been a mass alien abduction. "It's an easy place to get lost in," said my sister when I met her for only the second time in a quarter century.

The first was at the Suffolk County Jail in Riverhead after the FBI found and arrested her and extradited her to New York for trial nearly two decades into her life on the run. All along she had been here in Ohio, little more than an hour south of Columbus, where my mother's mother was born in 1902 and where her father's people had settled as landowners and traders and farmers and storekeepers on their migration west from Virginia.

During those missing years I had filled in with imagination what I lacked in fact and sometimes joked with friends about Laura being my own Patty Hearst. But she was not some kind of brainwashed revolutionary, not the Tania of the Symbionese Liberation Army looking to liberate anyone from "racism, sexism, ageism, capitalism, fascism, individualism, possessiveness, competitiveness and all other such institutions that have made and sustained capitalism." She was my wayward little sister who had made some awful decisions.

"I got caught up," she said now in the restaurant. Maybe it was no more complicated than that. Back when the rest of us in high school were dropping acid and tripping to Dr. John or Hendrix or the Incredible String Band, Laura was already thick with the speed freaks and junkies, people who hid their hypodermic "outfits" in the seams of their Landlubber jeans; had already begun drifting in and out of separatist communes that were functionally closer to cults.

It is easier than you think, she said now, to fall off the grid.

And this occurred during the years after she vanished, disappearing with her husband and infant daughter to Ohio, living in one after another small town near the state's southern border with Kentucky, places where sheets hung across windows was one way to tell a place was a meth house, giving birth to three more children in under five years, changing names and identification papers, and moving whenever people got nosy.

We ordered dinner and drinks. I had a margarita, a strange choice I suppose in an Italian restaurant. She ordered coffee with three sugars and milk, and I understood from this and not anything she said that she was now sober. "For a while there, I was an apartment house for babies," Laura said. Those babies are now all adults.

During the early periods in hiding, when she was often pregnant—as Laura explained over a plate of barely touched pasta—her husband worked as a long-haul trucker with a sideline providing local sex workers with transportation. Laura was left alone for long stretches, secreted in first one then another rural community, none much farther than a half day by car from this farm-to-table bistro in Dayton's renovated historic district.

A waitress with old-time flash tattoos and a septum piercing refilled Laura's coffee, and I switched to white wine. It seemed improbable to me that a person wanted by both state and federal authorities could have lived so ordinary a life, but I did not mention this when—once the waitress was out of earshot—Laura said matter-of-factly that for years she had changed addresses an average of once every six months, and taken the kinds of jobs where people asked the fewest questions. She cleaned houses and waitressed and then eventually found work as a welder at a factory that made parts for windmills. It was the last job she held down before the police showed up at her trailer to arrest her for a crime that, although decades old, still fell within the statute of limitations.

By then, I learned, she was also farming seventy-two acres of undeveloped land, cultivating cannabis in a back field and raising hybrid wolf dogs, details that emerged not at dinner but on a drive we took together the following day. By undeveloped land she meant that there had been no paved roads or running water. For field irrigation there was a tube well. Potable water was bought in fifty-five-gallon tight-head drums and hauled home in the flatbed of an old Ford pickup.

At the time of Laura's disappearance the internet had not yet been invented. Through all her years on the run, she never once lifted a telephone receiver other than for calls arranged in advance. She was so much in the habit of walking with her head bent that a farmer she met pointed out that she'd get where she was going a lot quicker if she looked at things straight on.

"I loved it," Laura says of that time of her life. "It's probably the happiest I've ever been."

I asked how she got caught and she said she wasn't sure. Maybe it was a credit card check. Maybe someone ratted her out: "They don't exactly tell you who turned you in when you get caught."

Laura was tried and convicted and sentenced to five years in federal prison, first at the Bedford Hills Correctional Facility for Women and later in a maximum-security facility in upstate Auburn, New York.

She was matter-of-fact about what she was willing to share but said no more than needed. I did not see much point in probing further or even prolonging my stay.

"One thing I did learn in prison," Laura said brightly. "At least as kids we knew we were loved."

"Did we?"

"When you've been with people whose parents turned them out on the streets at ten or burned them with cigarettes or beat them or prostituted them as children," she replied, "you never take what we had for granted again."

Laura sat at dinner that evening with her back to the wall, propping the cane she used to walk in the corner of a bead-board wall. When it slid to the floor with a thud I asked what happened, and she explained that she'd had an accident on the job. Up until the previous summer she had worked at a local country club as an assistant manager and dining room hostess. The club was one of the fanciest and more socially exclusive in the area, she said, as though we were still back in the Long Island of our youth, cruising around in our father's Cadillac Coupe de Ville.

One morning at the club, as she headed to the basement early to get a jump on setup, she explained, she had balanced heavy metal ice buckets in the crook of each elbow and clutched a sleeve of Styrofoam cups under her chin. Elbowing the door open she slipped and slid down the dark steps in free fall, swiveling midair. As the buckets went flying, she came down hard on the concrete. For thirty minutes or more she lay in the dark with a shattered femur waiting for someone from the morning shift to arrive. "It's kind of a miracle I didn't bleed out internally," she said. Fishing in her handbag, she pulled out an X-ray showing the pins and plates holding her leg together.

"That looks bad," I said, casting my eye around for the server and the check. I felt somehow that the X-ray was her way of acknowledging what we both knew, that things get broken and heal but once shattered are never the same as they were. "I'm an Erector Set," Laura said.

Halloween was a few days off. The bistro—and what few going businesses there were in that part of town—occupied part of nineteenth-century industrial Dayton whose brick warehouses had been repurposed. One now housed a bar selling craft brews. One, a defunct movie palace, had been made over as a sex shop called Exotic Fantasies. A sign on the old marquee read: "Slip into Winter: We Got Lube."

Laura and I arranged to meet again the next day and stepped out into the chill black night. I found I was eager to return to my dismal hotel room with its twin beds and view of a parking lot outside a mall. I could not reconcile the image of the weary and hollow-eyed person I saw with a picture I have of Laura when young.

In that old snapshot from a birthday party we are seated on a lawn in dappled shade. It must have been her birthday because she is wearing a frilly party dress and tearing the wrapping paper off a present. I look at the photograph all the time on my desk as if to remind myself that Borges was right. It is not really events from the past we recall. It's the last time we remembered them.

A big holiday celebration was scheduled for the neighborhood the next night, Laura informed me as we parted. That explained all the skull garlands festooning storefronts, skeletons hung from lampposts by nooses.

"What's it called?" I asked.

"I forget," she says. "There's a poster for it in that bar window. Let's look."

We crossed the empty street, with Laura walking speedily ahead despite her limp.

"Oh, that's funny," she said when I caught up.

"What is it?"

"It's called 'Hauntfest.'"

o   o   o

IN 1975, the summer when my mother died, we spent a lot of time pretending. We pretended at first that she had not been given a fatal prognosis and she was being treated for a liver infection and then that there was nothing unusual about long-out-of-touch old friends turning up suddenly after many years to say hello. We pretended not to be terrified by the physical changes in our mother's appearance, her yellowed pupils and bloated legs, her frightening weight loss. By "we" I mean my father and myself. My younger siblings had been largely excluded from the facts for what I was encouraged to think was their own protection.

Officially speaking, even my mother was kept from the truth about her pancreatic cancer diagnosis and the further fact that she would be lucky to last another eight weeks.

Soon after confiding all this in me, my dad took us to a

Dairy Barn drive-through. He bought us ice cream sandwiches and parked behind it and sat wordlessly facing the fake barn siding. We chose to see *Jaws,* less for the film than for the reassurance of being in some neutral space, frozen in place by the arctic air-conditioning, with the yeasty buttery smell of popcorn surrounding us just as it had when we were kids and our mother took us to double features as a distraction from her marital isolation.

Though I strain to remember much about this stupid movie, I think my mom may have liked it. Somehow horror films never seemed to scare her. My mother failed pretty quickly and the urgency of sensing how little time there was produced a form of hysteria as we acted as though the strange things we were doing were normal. We ordered her favorite confections—anachronistic things like Nesselrode pie—and other things she could no longer stomach. We drove her to visit her best friend and left that poor woman to pretend that the two of them were sunning and tanning as though nothing were amiss on lawn chairs set by a pool where a sign on the gate read: "Welcome to Our 'Ool.' Notice There Is No 'P' in It. Let's Keep It That Way!"

When my mother could no longer leave the house, we brought cups of ice for her to sip on the living room sofa and placed boxes of Pall Mall cigarettes on the coffee table alongside her in fresh packs. Our plan had been to tend to her at home right up to the end. But it became clear that this was impossible when on one horrible afternoon she began clawing the air for breath. It had not occurred to me that the actual dying could happen so suddenly once it started. An ambulance was called then. She was transferred to the third floor of Huntington Hospital. And there, in a sunny private room with a view over a nearby park, she lay in a haze of morphine administered in a gentle drip, half in and half out of life.

For quite a long time I struggled with the rage I felt at her for leaving, seemingly hard to justify when you are talking about a vital forty-two-year-old facing her own death. Eventually I saw that the leave-taking was less the problem than her tacit agreement with the lie and a fiction that prevented her from saying a proper goodbye to us, her children.

Later on in life I will have ample experience of early death and will finally feel forgiveness for her and also for myself for keeping that ugly pact, the agreement to treat as immortal this skeletal wraith that had once been our hilarious and vivacious young mother, the prankster who chased us around the house to grab us and give us wrist burns, the daredevil girl who once thought nothing of racing into big surf.

Sometime during those final weeks I bought my mother a drugstore wristwatch. She hadn't wanted to wear the fancy one my father bought her years ago in Rome. Strapped tight to her emaciated forearm, the Timex looked ridiculous. What use did she have anymore for a device to mark the remaining hours and minutes?

I still have the Timex. I keep it along with whatever you might term my important papers in a safe-deposit box in a bank vault below East Seventy-Second Street in Manhattan. Every November around my mother's birthday I make an appointment to go there and rummage through the box's contents. Banks were important structures when we were kids, as imposing and monumental as a church or a courthouse. Now, of course, they are mostly fluorescent-lit vestibules with withdrawal slips littering the floor.

The bank branch I patronize is an old-style cathedral to lucre, however, with a marble entry, fluted mahogany columns, terrazzo floors, and a paneled stair leading down to the vaults. On my last visit there, I waited for an officer to conduct me to the vault where the safe-deposit boxes are stored, drifting into a cubicle where a book had been left on a desk. The book was a translation into French of a deeply troubling tale about New York gay life in the 1980s. On its cover was a close-up photograph showing the face of a man in what appears to be the throes of agony but was, in fact, orgasm.

The man who shot that picture, my friend Peter Hujar, died a long time back. I was ruminating about him when the bank officer arrived and waved me down a stair leading to a subterranean sign-in desk. There we conducted the registration formalities and he led me through an elaborately locked ornamental grille door with, beyond it, the large vault where banks of boxes were arranged in order by size. Some were the size of mini-refrigerators.

What treasures must they contain? Some, like mine, were narrow, small, and oblong and could only be reached using a rolling ladder that the bank officer climbed to unlock using a master key and the matching one I held, then sliding the box out of its slot.

I idly asked how often these box spaces became available. "Never, really," he said. "Well, I mean, there's a waiting list, but it's more than ten years."

Carrying the box, I followed him into a walnut-paneled hall surrounded by doors leading to small privacy cubicles.

"Take whichever one you want," he said, and I chose booth 5 because the number feels auspicious and also because my visit here was nothing if not ceremonial and superstitious.

Two rolling chairs faced a leather-covered desk lighted from beneath, a single desk lamp the only other illumination in the room. Sliding the oblong metal box across the counter, I methodically emptied it of its contents: a stiffened manila envelope containing my birth certificate, hole-punched passports expired and canceled; a childhood bankbook with punch-stamped entries in amounts of one dollar or five dollars or ten.

A small baize-lined tray held a knot of ladies' rings, some random gold junk, a set of shirt studs, and a pair of Orson Foster's cuff links in the form of miniature knots. There was a ring with three entwined branches terminating in a stone from each of Lucy Foster's marriages. Because the box lid was hinged at the three-quarter point, it was necessary to run my hand around the inside to find everything, and distracted briefly, I lost track of my point in being there until my fingers touched the edge of the envelope containing the watch and the list.

I slipped the Timex out onto the leather-topped counter. Its hands had stopped long ago on some indeterminate day at 3:00. I became aware of the sound of my own breath, my slowing pulse, a feeling that people had begun to crowd into the cubicle with me and that was what I had come for because in that box I found a roster of all those I've lost, the ghosts I might otherwise forget. The safe-deposit box is my place of last addresses.

It's far from a gloomy errand, so much as it is my way of breaking the taboo on naming the dead. I may not call their names, as in a mourner's Kaddish, but as I tabulate them mentally I invoke the love I hold for my ghosts as a proxy for a God I have no use for. I sit as I did that day in that quiet cubicle and invoke people like sexy cantankerous Peter Hujar and all the many men in those Super 8 films we made in the mid-seventies, such ones as I know have died, and the heroic friends met then and taken as their adult lives were starting, people whose valor and terror I can never forget; and also Candy Darling with her missing cap; and beautiful Robert Yoh, the model who, after he knew he was going to die, washed down several dozen Seconals with vodka and killed himself first, leaving behind instructions that his ashes were to be buried in a pet cemetery beneath a headstone reading "Man's Best Friend."

I thought that day of Cookie Mueller at the funeral for her husband, Vittorio Scarpati, who died in September of 1989 from the effects of the HIV that, two months later, would also claim Cookie herself at forty—not, however, before the onset of dementia, pneumonia, and a stroke that immobilized one side of her body. I recalled Cookie's speaking voice, at odds with her tough-girl demeanor, and her tendency to talk as if in movie dialogue. I recalled Cookie chiding someone at Vittorio's funeral to stop blubbering: "Oh, hon, it's only the body that goes," said Cookie. "The spirit lives eternally."

I did not cry in booth 5 as I read a list of nearly one hundred names, relatives and friends who constitute a separate personal genealogy, and I laid the cheap little wristwatch with its webbed nylon strap across my palm and drifted back in memory to the placid summer light falling through the window of my mother's hospital room. I allowed myself to think that sometimes even as life destroys us it brings solace. And remembered how, many years after my mother died, I found myself at a voguing ball in Harlem, there to receive an honorary recognition plaque from the mothers and fathers of the venerable House of Ultra Omni.

It was a typical ball in a hellhole in the middle of winter, scum ice blackening the gutter along Third Avenue and patrons crowded together for warmth as they lined up on the sidewalk and inched toward the ticket taker at the door. Up a rickety stair was a barnlike loft filled with people crowding around rented tables and contestants turning bathrooms and hallways into impromptu dressing rooms.

And I remember Willi Ninja, most truly legendary of all the voguers, shy as always, greeting me with a hug. I had no way of knowing it at the time, but Willi would be dead in under a month, age forty-five. I remembered how pleased Willi seemed that it was he who'd be presenting me with my plaque commending me, with the counterlogic of the ballroom children, as "An Icon—for Withholding Significance for 25 Years."

Far from having withheld significance, I had sought to record it in my own make-do fashion. Certainly the places in which I chose to look for it—rubble lots in the South Bronx, the ramparts of an ancient Muslim graveyard in Old Delhi, at the ballrooms themselves—were often unlikely. Willi whispered that he was dedicating his runway walk to me, a performance that finally took place at two or maybe three a.m. and that seemed more than ever feverish and inspired and fearsome as Willi walked and dipped and pantomimed, throwing shade on anyone delusional enough to think he could be vanquished on a dance floor.

o   o   o

AFTER LONG HOURS spent at my mother's bedside, my father and siblings were in need of a break. For no reason I can any longer recall I offered to stay behind. My mother was by then in some ambiguous state, some distant realm of consciousness. Faint tremors flickered across her shuttered eyelids like cat's paws on water. I reached across the crisp sheets to hold her hand and watched her breathing, and it seemed to me she had gone far away, as though she had been pulled underwater and was trying to regain the surface. Since lapsing into a coma she had said nothing, uttered not a word, and so I was scared as much as startled when suddenly she clutched my hand with tremendous primal strength and spoke her last words: "Do something."

There in the bank vault with the list in my hand, I turned this phrase over and over again. Imploring, urgent, exhorting, I can never hope to know its meaning. I returned the watch to the box, shut the lid, and handed it to the waiting banker, who stowed it in the appropriate niche and fastened the door with both keys, returning mine to me in its stiff paper snap-sleeve.

A grille door shut behind me as I climbed the stairs to the street. It was a time of year when the days had begun to contract and there was about the late-autumn light something clean and absolving. Silently, then I replied to her, as I also had before: "I will try. Mother, know that."

Acknowledgments

Initiated over a Monkey Bar lunch, forged in a cyclone on the East Coast Road in Tamil Nadu as our little Toyota bashed through gale-force winds and lashing rain, my relationship with my extraordinary agent, Lynn Nesbit, has been, in every sense, a trip. Were it not for her fierce loyalty and support, this book may never have come into existence. And its writing has relied throughout on the unswerving guidance of my editor, Erroll McDonald, whose counsel set my compass. My gratitude to each is immeasurable.

I would like also to thank those who gave me a place in which to write, foremost Paula Madden, who, time and again, shared her hospitality and, in countless subtle ways, came to my assistance. I am deeply indebted as well to Patricia Brennan and Muriel Trebay Brennan; Adrienne E. Harris; Holland Goss Lynch and Michèle Goss; Meenakshi Meyyappan; and Todd A. Romano for sheltering me variously in Milford, Pennsylvania; Napa, California; Sag Harbor, New York; Karaikudi, India; and Newport, Rhode Island; and to Cathy B. Graham for offering me a perch among the treetops of East Seventy-Eighth Street.

I would like to thank Debe Cuevas Lykes, Allison Fleming, and the directors, past and present, of Stratford Hall for their unstinting hospitality, and I am grateful as well to the trustees of the John Jermain Memorial Library in Sag Harbor for their commitment to maintaining one of the cornerstones of a civilized society: a public library.

Robin Desser was the first to see the possibilities of this book, and I am thankful for her foresight, as well as to the late Sonny Mehta, Reagan Arthur, and the teams at both Janklow & Nesbit Associates and Alfred A. Knopf for shepherding this book with patience and care—and, in the case of Cassandra Pappas and Chip Kidd, elevating it through their designs. Thank you, Hannah Davey, Michael Steger, and Mina Hamedi at Janklow & Nesbit and Nicholas Latimer, Kathryn Zuckerman, Belinda Yong, and Brian Etling at Knopf.

So many friends have helped along the way, carrying me through with acts of generosity small and large. I would like to thank André Aciman, Renata Adler, Tanya Akim, Hilton Als, Vince Aletti, Jon Robin Baitz, Bimla Bissell, Catherine Gerlach Blair, Holly Brubach, Tina Brown, Marie Brenner, William Polk Carey, Cynthia Carr, Yolanda Cuomo, Joan Didion, Shelagh Doyle, Christopher E. Franklin, Carol Friedman, Fabrice Gili, Perry Pidgeon Hooks, Gary Indiana, Jeff Klein, Eric Konigsberg, Peter L. Kopelson, Brigitte Lacombe, Ruth La Ferla, Elena Echarte Lord, Ned Lord, Rob Morea, Donald Moss, Eric P. Neibart, Kipp Nelson, Nancy G. Novogrod, Tracy Roe, Marianne Rohrlich, Geoff Shandler, Sheila Donnelly Theroux, Judith Thurman, Kathryn Nelson Urban, Mim Udovitch, Clara Vannucci, Stellene Volandes, Susan

Wiviott, Hanya Yanagihara, Simona and Claudio Zampa, Lynne Zeavin, and Paula Hyman Zukor.

Additionally, I owe a debt of gratitude to colleagues past and present—Rosemary Kent at *Interview,* Alexandra Anderson, Karen Durbin, Jonathan Z. Larsen, M Mark, Marianne Partridge-Poett, and David Schneiderman at *The Village Voice* for seeing in me things I could not, in many cases, see in myself. I thank my dear friend of decades Sylvia Plachy for being—sometimes literally—my ride-or-die. And I would like to thank among the colleagues of my two decades at *The New York Times* Stella Bugbee, Trip Gabriel, Anita Leclerc, Joseph Lelyveld, Minju Pak, Stefano Tonchi, and Sam Sifton.

Readers of this book are bound to come away with a sense of mine as having been a deeply fragmented family. Yet, for all my parents' apparent carelessness, there was a core of love, and I am grateful to them, as also to my late sister, Dana, my brother Glenn and sister Laura, who will, I hope, find compassion for this version of a story we shared. I am not much in the habit of quoting Freud. Yet, in a letter he once wrote to Wilhelm Fliess (Leo Bersani, *Thoughts and Things,* Chicago: University of Chicago Press, 2014, page 69), the founder of modern psychotherapy observed—correctly, as it happens— that the past, never really lost, is subject to multiple retranscriptions. This book, then, is mine.

Finally, deep thanks to Kate Tentler, who stuck by me steadfastly through the years it took to write this, cheering me to the finish line.

A NOTE ON THE TYPE

This book was set in Granjon, a type named in comple-
ment to Robert Granjon, a type cutter and printer active in
Antwerp, Lyon, Rome, and Paris from 1523 to 1590. Granjon, the boldest and most original designer of his time, was
one of the first to practice the trade of typefounder apart
from that of printer.

Linotype Granjon was designed by George W. Jones,
who based his drawings on a face used by Claude Garamond (ca. 1480–1561) in his beautiful French books. Granjon more closely resembles Garamond's own type than do
any of the various modern faces that bear his name.

Composed by North Market Street Graphics,
Lancaster, Pennsylvania

Printed and bound by Berryville Graphics,
Berryville, Virginia

Designed by Cassandra J. Pappas